C000281279

BREAK THE MOULD

VOLUME 1

How to be *your* best version of you

TIM ROBERTS

Copyright © 2022

Published by Known Publishing, 2022

The right of Tim Roberts to be identified as the Author of the Work has
been asserted by him in accordance with the Copyright, Designs and
Patents Act 1988. All rights reserved.

Paperback: 978-1-913717-78-0

Hardback: 978-1-913717-75-9

Ebook: 978-1-913717-72-8

This book is sold subject to the condition it shall not, by way of trade
or otherwise, be circulated in any form or by any means, electronic or
otherwise without the publisher's prior consent.

www.get-known.co.uk

PRAISE FOR
BREAK THE MOULD

"This book is pure heart on a sleeve. And right at the centre sits a very important question; leadership or leader-shit? You already know the answer, but finally, we have a book that shows us how."

**– GAVIN OATTES, BEST-SELLING AUTHOR
& INTERNATIONAL SPEAKER**

"Put your hands together for the best fucking book in the world!"

– MATTHEW BRENNON, TIM'S BEST MATE

"Disarmingly witty, original, and practical, this is the must-read for any leader genuinely serious about futureproofing themselves and teams. The author's original no-bullshit style makes for a refreshingly empowering take on leadership and business."

**– JULIA DARVILL, INSPIRATIONAL LEADER
& GENERAL MANAGER, PURATOS UK**

"There are 100s of reasons to love Tim, but one that I value the most is how he is unapologetic in being himself, his lack of interest in dancing the dance of corporate bullshit

is a joy to be around. As a gift to Tim, I end with a quote, one that I think Tim embeds every minute of the day 'Be you, everybody else is taken'. Thanks for being you Tim."

– DANNY SEALS, INTERNATIONAL MAN OF
MYSTERY AKA EXPERIENCE DESIGN GENIUS

"I knew Tim in his brown shoe days, and also when he was trying to fit into the mould. I'll tell you a secret, Tim's nickname then was 'boring' (he knew about this nickname, and we laughed about it?!). I met Tim a few years later when he had decided to ditch the bullshit and be himself and wow what a change. Tim lives his values, has broke the mould, found himself and as a result he's doing some amazing things. If you do the same, this book can literally CHANGE YOUR LIFE."

– ZOE JONES, PEOPLE & CULTURE LEAD (AND ONE OF THE LEAST
DICKHEAD PEOPLE TIM HAS EVER WORKED WITH)

"If you are a leader that wants to be more authentic by being your best you and being comfortable being you, then this book is for you! It's a modern take on Leadership complete with modern-day language, fresh current examples complete with a smattering of great music lyrics… What's not to like?! Be yourself, cut through the crap and in a post covid world connect on your own level. Break the mould!"

– STEVE SMITH, TEAM GB OLYMPIC MEDALLIST
AND FOUNDER OF RAISE THE BAR LTD

"I've never read a leadership book like this. It's so far from any (boring) leadership book I've ever read that I don't even know what category I'd put it in. Either the 'this book will save your soul' category or the 'don't you dare go to work until you've read this book' category."

– AIMEE BATEMAN, ENTREPRENEUR & SPEAKER (AND CHIEF OF KICKER OF TIM'S ARSE WHEN HE NEEDS IT!)

"As expected, Tim's book is a refreshing, no-nonsense perspective on leadership… it's a leadership book like no other… He has absolutely broken the mould, calling out all that is wrong about leadership… he shares his personal experiences, in a no-nonsense and humorous way, bringing to life what really matters… how to be your best version of you. Tim writes like he speaks… he's engaging, authentic and seriously knows his stuff. He epitomises zero BS. This book isn't for you if you're offended by the truth, colourful language, warts and all. Where else have you had a chance to reflect on your 'circle of nobheads!' and your 'no moan zone!'. Using music lyrics to resonate and inspire, Tim's book aims to truly sing to both your heart and mind."

– JO WRIGHT, CEO COACHING CULTURE

"You have all heard the quote 'If you love what you do you will never work a day in your life' – more than anyone I know, Tim is the man who lives, breathes and owns this philosophy. His passion and unique, direct and bullshit-free Leadership beliefs and principles shine through on every page of the book. Hang on to your hats!"

– ROB JOHNSON, LEADERSHIP COACH AND TIM'S MENTOR

"If you're not a dickhead, and would like to succeed in your career without morphing into one, you could really do with a Tim - or at least this book!

I can see myself dipping in and out of this book for years to come! As someone who's worked with Tim (and benefited enormously), Break The Mould is just about the next best thing to having him on hand 24/7 to give you a nudge when any aspect of leadership starts to feel particularly difficult, uncomfortable, or at conflict with who you truly are.

Any position where you're leading people will always come with it's challenges - no book will ever magically make leadership easy - but what Break The Mould will do, is show you why - and how - leading as your authentic self will give you increased clarity and confidence in your decisions and approach, getting you out of your own way."

– BETHANY LANG, PEOPLE DIRECTOR

A note from my family:

"I have seen the blood, sweat and tears that Tim has put into this book. If it helps you as much as he wants it to and as much as how hard he has worked on writing it then it will all be worth it. He talks a lot about nobheads in here and (sometimes) he is the biggest nobhead going!... but he's our nobhead."

– LYNN ROBERTS (JOYNO), TIM'S BETTER HALF

"We're very proud of you Daddy and you are an inspiration. If this book is half as good as your trumps are smelly, then it will be a bestseller!"

– PHOEBE AND LUCIE, TIM'S DAUGHTERS,
AND BIGGEST SOURCE OF INSPIRATION

This book is dedicated to

Joyno, Pheebs, Lucie & Dusty.

Love you all the world.

Keep smiling. Keep being you.

CONTENTS

PART ONE:
THE DANGERS OF FITTING THE MOULD ...37

PART TWO:
HOW TO BREAK THE MOULD AND BE
THE BEST VERSION OF YOU ...169

In better times, you will fly

Do all the things you wanna do

Not all the things that others want you to

So, what you need, is to see

It's okay to be yourself

And that with belief

That the world will do the rest

Ah, belief, and the world will do the rest.

– PAUL WELLER

THIS BOOK IS FOR...

The easy way to finish that sentence is with 'you'. This book is for you. It's for you because it always starts with you.

➡ Are you fed up with corporate bullshit?

➡ Do you know there is a different way to lead but don't yet know where to start?

➡ Have you had enough of being micromanaged?

➡ Do you want to be less stressed?

➡ Are you sick of being sent on the same useless training sessions?

➡ Do you want to be excited about the impact you'll make on others?

➡ Would you like to wake up on a Monday morning feeling like you actually want to go to work?

This book is for the leaders at every level who feel trapped in the corporate mould and want to break free and be their authentic selves – not the person someone else wants them to be. It's for the leaders who are currently battling company culture, bad bosses and a lack of role models, all while being worn down by the same old shit.

It's for those leaders who perhaps don't yet know where to start, who are not sure if it's possible or even if they're allowed to be their authentic selves. The leaders who think it's their organisations or other people who need to change. The leaders who are struggling with leadership because they know there is a different way and that it's meant to feel different. The leaders who are scared to step out and be different, knowing in their heart that they want to do it but not how to do it just yet.

You don't need to be a particular type of leader or have a certain title or level of experience. The book isn't for your job title; it doesn't matter whether you're a CEO with 30 years' experience or not even a leader yet. As long as you are a decent human being, then this book is for you and will show you how to get what you really want from your job while remaining true to yourself.

THIS BOOK WILL...

Make authentic leadership go from something you admire in others to something you do effortlessly every day. If you've been waiting for permission to change, then this book is it! It's going to free you from the confines of the moulds that others have made for you, even if you don't know about them yet, and it will allow you to become the best version of you.

As a result of reading this book, you're going to be your true, authentic self. You're going to be a confident leader. You're going to break the mould. To do that, I'll take you on a journey through the realities of leadership, showing you that it always starts with you – you need to sort your own shit out before you can start leading others. I'll share the story of how I went from stressed-out, unhappy leader to doing what I love, and I'll tell you about all the bumps along the way – like getting bollocked for wearing the wrong colour shoes, and getting punched in the face by a young girl in my team. I'll share lots of inspirational stories with you, and I'll point out the dickheads along the way; there's always some dickhead that you'll have to deal with. Everything I share with you will make you think, showing you how to choose a positive response to your thoughts and feelings. After all, being guided by what's important to you and those around you is key, allowing you to drop the bullshit and ignore the preconceptions so you can lead in the real world.

Once you've read this book, you will have fully left behind the legions of leaders who toe the line and do what everyone else does, no matter how miserable it makes them, and you will actually be yourself.

I will show you that you don't need someone else's theory, model or style of leadership; what you really need is you. Guess what? That's what the people you lead really want anyway, and when you realise that, it becomes so much easier, making leadership a win-win. Wherever you are at right now as a leader, by the end of the book you will have dropped the preconceptions of what you need to do or be as 'someone's boss' and you will only be concerned with being what you and everyone else needs you to be: yourself.

If you don't know how to do that yet, this book will give you lots of practical ideas for how you can break the mould. Once you've sorted yourself out, it will then show you how to supercharge the way you lead and positively influence others. It will develop your emotional intelligence and enhance your ability to self-coach. From reading this book, you will understand how to build value-adding relationships and stop wasting your time and energy on the wrong things – people who want you to fit the mould – by showing you how it always starts with you and then goes out to others.

If you've bought this book expecting to learn lots of new leadership skills, then put it down and go and subscribe to LinkedIn Learning or sign up for the latest training courses at work. Breaking the mould isn't about skills. It's about making positive choices– the choices you already have the ability to make. That's what this book will do for you: it will help you to break the mould by showing you how to make positive choices to be the leader you want to be.

Before you go any further with this book, I want you to accept something: you could quit your job tomorrow, and someone else would come along and replace you. Your job is not you – you are you. I am going to help you to stick to that and find the happiness that you want in being a leader, which is what made you take the job in the first place.

Breaking the mould will make you your best version of you.

Let's get you breaking the mould...

You can only be true to yourself.

– PAUL WELLER

HOW TO USE THIS BOOK

Firstt things first – read it! You've paid your money or been given it as a gift, so you might as well take your chances and actually read it.

As you read it, pay attention to the questions I ask you. Get into the habit of writing down the thoughts and ideas that the book sparks for you. The most important thing you can do to help you to understand how to use this book is to ask yourself, 'What am I going to do about it?' and identify the positive choices you would make as a result of investing your time and energy into reading the book.

Clear your mind of all the bullshit and preconceptions of what leadership is or what you have to do because your job or boss tells you to do it. Don't worry about all the leadership styles, models and theories. Use the book for a bit of escapism; read it for 15 minutes in between your boring meetings and video calls and use it to make you think. Think about who you really are and what leadership really means to you and those around you. Use it to laugh at the dickheads and take pride in the fact that you are not going to be like them.

Get the Break the Mould *workbook*

To really get the most out of this book, make sure you head to my learning resource website to get a *Break the Mould* workbook, which will help you to use what you have read and not just leave it as 'another leadership book' on your shelf. Get one now from **www.italwaysstartswithyou.com.**

The workbook shows you how to do the great work in this book in the real world. The book will get you started, while the workbook will help you to continue on your journey towards breaking the mould. What I will make you think about and ask you to do in each chapter will get you going; the workbook takes it to the next level and shows you how to do it with your team.

In the workbook, you get:

➡ A planner to check in with yourself every day, targeting how you will break the mould

➡ Self-coaching questions to use every day

➡ Questions for each chapter of the book to help you choose what you are going to do about it

➡ Space to capture your thoughts and self-reflections

➡ Worked examples of all the ideas in this book, with real-life demonstrations

➡ Exclusive video content that you can watch on demand when you need a reminder for how to break the mould

➡ Additional resources for how you can break the mould with your team, including:

- A worksheet for creating your and your team's Map of the World

- Your No-Moan Zone sign

- A Circle of Nobheads worksheet

- Tips on how to ask powerful open questions

- Advice on how to really listen

By using the workbook, both while reading and long after you've finished, your team will take care of their own performance and behaviours, your team communication will improve and your meetings will run on track and not be a total moanfest. You will create and lead a team of true, authentic people– an idea that is super powerful. You will make your days better by adding humour into the drudgery of work. You will make sure that you never get trapped by the corporate bullshit and write your very own dickhead prevention insurance policy. Inspirational leaders are those who break the mould for themselves first and then help others to do it too. That's what the *Break the Mould* work-book will do for you.

A lot of the resources I've included have taken me years to develop and fine-tune. I use parts of this workbook with my corporate clients when I'm delivering training. It's worth thousands to them, but I'm letting you have it for only a tenner – *plus* you'll get a £10 voucher towards my next tour, effectively making it free. Talk about a no-brainer!

Get it now from **www.italwaysstartswithyou.com** to make sure your journey towards being your best version of you continues long after you've finished reading the book.

Scan the code below to purchase your digital workbook:

MEET TIM ROBERTS

Tim Roberts is:

➡ A husband, father, and Mod before anything else

➡ A leadership coach who created Enthuse Coaching in 2018 to help people to be their best version of themselves

➡ Sick of the dickheads

➡ One of the most engaging and popular inspirational speakers in the UK. Seriously, book him before you finish reading this book to make sure you don't miss out!

➡ Here to coach you to make positive choices

He has:

➡ Inspired thousands of people to be their true, authentic selves

➡ A firmly held belief that It Always Starts With You

➡ Learned (sometimes the hard way!) that Emotional Intelligence will get you further in life than anything else

➡ A unique no bullshit approach to coaching & leadership development

➡ Had enough of decent people being forced to fit the moulds that others set for them

Get in touch with Tim & subscribe at:

www.enthusecoaching.com

Follow Tim on social:

🔗 **www.linkedin.com/in/timrobertsenthuse/**

🐦 **@TimRoberts78**

PREFACE:
THIS IS A CORPORATE-
BULLSHIT-FREE ZONE

Where we're going; this shit don't matter.

– GERRY CINNAMON

'Hi, Tim. Can I see you for five minutes – will you come up to my office?'

I was summoned to my boss's boss's office. I dropped everything and off I went.

As I made the walk to the sacred part of the building where all of the big bosses had their offices, my emotions ranged from excitement to nerves, to trying to think if I'd done anything wrong.

At first, I thought *this is it; my time has come.* I was going to be asked to work on a big project, or asked for my advice, or asked to help on a senior leadership issue. I was well thought of and had been waiting for my invite into the inner sanctum with the big bosses.

But as I got nearer to her office, a sense of impending doom came over me. I started to think I'd done something wrong, and the anxiety and dread increased with every step. By the time I got to her door, it was like I'd gone back to being a 10-year-old boy approaching the headmaster's office.

I knocked and was beckoned to come inside, close the door and sit down.

Close the door, I thought. *Must be important!*

I waited in anticipation for what was so important for me: the chance to get a private audience with the boss.

And then she said it. 'I need to talk to you about your shoes, Tim.'

'OK,' I stammered, looking down at them. 'Erm, what about my shoes?'

'Why are you wearing brown shoes?'

At this point, I drifted off. It was like one of those movie scenes where someone is talking and the other person can see their lips moving but all they can hear is their own thoughts.

What is she on about? My shoes? I thought this was some really important meeting, I brought my notepad and everything, and she's going on about my shoes? Is this actually happening?

She continued to waffle on, telling me how the dress code had been updated and it was now clear that managers are expected to wear only black or blue shoes to go with the blue company suit we were given as our uniform.

And then came the bit that really got my attention: the reason we were having this awkward conversation was because the CEO's PA had emailed my boss's boss to tell her I was wearing brown shoes, and could she speak to me because the CEO didn't know who I was, only that I worked in one of her teams.

By that stage, she had completely lost me and, for the next few minutes, I just sat there nodding and pursing my lips together at the right time to show acknowledgement.

And I don't dig what you gotta say.

– HAPPY MONDAYS

At the end of the one-way conversation, I walked out of her office with my head down, thinking *the colour of my shoes won't make me a better leader.*

You are who you are – no decent human being was ever created from corporate bullshit.

My 'I need to talk to you about your shoes' incident is a classic example of Class A Corporate Bullshit. Of another leader trying too hard to fit the mould that others made for her.

At that moment I saw the light. It became very clear to me that this organisation, to which I had given years of my career and for which I had worked such long hours, didn't care about me at all.

What they did care about was a superficial appearance that had no impact on my attitude or performance. Just for the record – my shoes were a pair of very cool brown lace-up leather brogues. It's not like I was wearing socks and sliders with a suit!

They were happy to take the credit for the excellent performance of my team, but what I got in return was grief about my shoes.

It's corporate bullshit at its best:

Updated dress code issued that no one is told about

+

Anal-retentive CEO who lacks the integrity to get to know the people who work for him

=

Awkward conversation between a self-preserving director and a subordinate, wasting their time and damaging their relationship

It demonstrates how corporate bullshit can seep out across an organisation – how many people does it take to tell someone they're wearing the wrong shoes? And why does the colour of their shoes even matter in the first place? It only matters because somebody somewhere at some point decided that brown shoes didn't fit the mould they had decided to set for everyone else.

From that moment on, I decided enough was enough. Never again was I going to put up with corporate bull-shit. And never again was I going to be suffocated by their utter disregard for what was really important. I was going to break the mould.

My brown shoes made me realise that you are who you are. Only you can be you. You are not the gear that you wear, you are not what you look like or the job you do. You are not even your thoughts and feelings. You are something much deeper and more meaningful than that. You are not born to fit into someone else's mould. You are YOU.

I realised that, to be the leader I wanted to be, I had to fight back against corporate bullshit. Corporate bullshit is why it's so hard to be unique and authentic. Supporting corporate bullshit forces square pegs into round holes, kills creativity and destroys our soul!

And if you hate it as much as I do, then this is the book for you.

Bullshit is bullshit;
it just goes by different names.

– THE JAM

I hate corporate bullshit because it stifles us and goes against all the reasons why we go to work in the first place:

➡ To do engaging and productive work

➡ To collaborate with inspirational people and inspire others

➡ To feel part of something and to contribute to achieving a shared purpose

➡ To have positive social interaction with like-minded people

When the 'why do you want to work here?' question gets asked at interview, no one ever answers:

➡ Because I want to go home feeling pissed off

➡ Because I love being patronised and feeling excluded

➡ Because I really like other people taking the credit for my hard work

➡ Because I want to get told off for wearing the wrong colour shoes

Corporate bullshit is what turns you from a loving parent and husband into a cantankerous, whingeing sod (trust me, I've been there).

Corporate bullshit tells you to fit into a mould and say and do the right thing according to someone else, turning you into a version of you that someone else wants you to be.

Leadership is about being the right thing and being your best version of you.

It never happens for people like us, you know. You know nothing ever happened on its own.

– THE ENEMY

Having policies and codes of conduct is OK; they keep people safe and set standards. You can't control the policies and codes of conduct. What you *can* control is you and how you lead yourself and others.

My boss's boss could have spent time getting to know me before she had to lambast me about my shoes. Had she got to know me, she could have been really candid with me about it and convinced me to buy some new ones for work and save my cool brown brogues for 'best'. Or, even better, she could have been proactive, sharing the new dress code when it was published and talking to her teams about why it was important for us to role model the right approach to the company uniform.

Instead, she was reactive and only chose to have the conversation because someone else told her to. The hilarious thing is that she didn't even wear the company uniform herself because her pay grade meant she didn't have to – what a great way to role model what you want from others! And because she hid behind some corporate bullshit, it made me even more determined to wear my brown shoes every day. They became my way of 'sticking it to the man'.

That's what corporate bullshit and reactive behaviour does to people. My boss's boss didn't get up that morning wanting to go to work to discuss my shoes. 'Sticking it to the man' is not something I believe in – or at least not without a proper cause to believe in, like injustice in society or discrimination at work. This was just about my shoes!

It always starts with you and the choices that you make. I want you to join me on a quest to destroy corporate bullshit and break the mould. Let's take a journey together to learn more about you and what you stand for, so you can be the leader that you and those around you want you to be.

You don't have to take this crap.
You don't have to sit back and relax.
You can actually try changing it.

– THE STYLE COUNCIL

PART ONE

THE DANGERS OF
FITTING THE MOULD

INTRODUCTION
TO PART ONE

In the first part of the book, I am going to tell you what breaking the mould is and why it is important. This part highlights the problem with trying to fit the mould and be someone you are not. It raises your awareness of what it is like to fit the mould, and the dangers of doing so.

It doesn't pull any punches and takes a no-bullshit approach to the realities of leadership, as reflected in some of my personal experiences. It shows you that it always starts with you, and it ends with my own story of what happened to me when I broke the mould.

In the good times and the bad times; people will remember you for how you behave.

What is breaking the mould?

It is how you make positive choices to be your true, authentic self. Not who other people tell you to be – breaking the mould means you can be who you want to be. Breaking the mould means you stop relying on leadership approaches that don't work. Instead, you start with you and put your time and energy into the only thing you are always 100% in control of: how you choose to respond to your thoughts and feelings.

Breaking the mould means you can win over what you're really up against as a leader: your emotions. You're not up against targets and deadlines, or getting promoted or your team getting results. You're not even up against your competitors. You're up against your own emotions, because they trigger your thoughts and feelings, and it's those thoughts and feelings that tell you to conform and fit the mould.

When you break the mould, you stop reacting to your perception of your situations and what you think people expect of you. Leaders who fit the mould believe they have to do everything that their thoughts and feelings tell them to do. When you break the mould, you choose a positive response to your thoughts and feelings and become who you really want to be.

**No change, I can change
I can change, I can change
But I'm here in my mould
I am here in my mould
But I'm a million different people
from one day to the next
I can change my mould.**

– THE VERVE

Leaders in the mould

The world is full of leaders who have given up and chosen to fit the mould. They choose to fit the mould because they are used to doing things in a particular way and can't muster the courage or energy to do things differently. They've given up because they're surrounded by other people who have given up, and so they fit the mould, allowing their thoughts and feelings to tell them what they can and can't do. They fit the mould because doing what everyone else does is easy. Doing nothing is easy. Doing the same thing over and over is easy. Moaning about something is easy. Blaming others is easy.

You know the types I am talking about. The ones who:

➡ Plod along in their leadership role, frustrating everyone with their blatant inertia

➡ Sit in the same meetings day after day without contributing

➡ Don't listen

➡ Take everything personally

➡ Do everything themselves, never delegating or trusting others to do it... and then complain about how busy they are

➡ Talk absolute bullshit instead of just saying it as it is

➡ Laugh at their boss's inappropriate jokes just because it's the boss

➡ Think they know it all

➡ Are passive-aggressive

➡ Kiss the arse of the owners or senior leaders

➡ Think they run the company (get over yourself!)

➡ Hide behind a corporate mask

➡ Are really disorganised and make others stressed

➡ Build no rapport with anyone

➡ Convince themselves that nothing will ever change... although they spend half their time moaning about what needs to change

➡ Don't reply to emails but then demand a reply from you the second they send one

➡ Always cry 'I'm too busy'

➡ Only ever talk about work stuff

➡ Lack empathy

➡ Work long hours because they think it makes them look busy and important

➡ Only focus on the negatives and pick up on every mistake that their team make

➡ Keep attending leadership development courses, although they do nothing as a result

➡ Have zero self-awareness

Leaders who fit the mould do what everyone else tells them to do. They rely on their technical competence and authority and lose sight of the human element of leadership, even though it conflicts with who they really are and what they stand for. They fail to evolve. They react to their emotions

"Leaders who fit the mould do what everyone else tells them to do. They lose sight of the human element of leadership" and go on unintentional autopilot, guided by negative thoughts and feelings. They are the mood hoovers who populate every organisation's payroll. Typical traits of a leader who fits the mould include:

➡ Snapping at their team

➡ Openly criticising other people

➡ Creating a blame culture

➡ Being in self-preservation mode

➡ Lacking self-confidence

➡ Facing constant internal doubts (and using bravado to cover them up)

➡ Never 'walking the walk'

➡ Being a miserable, unapproachable bastard

In other words, they are all of the things that no one wants to be. Yet thousands of leaders allow themselves to become exactly what they don't want to be.

One of the biggest problems that leads to managers fitting the mould is when they try to copy other managers' style and approach. So many people (including the younger me) try to channel what other people do and think that it is how you lead. The problem with that approach is that you can never ever take full responsibility or be accountable for your own attitudes and behaviours when you are simply copying others. If you start to follow the lead of others, then when it doesn't work, you are exposed as a fraud and you're left looking to others because 'that's how they do it'. However, they will be nowhere to be seen when you try to imitate them and fail as a result.

Organisations are full of moulds created by senior or long-serving managers that make others think they have to behave that way and that their attitude is the one to adopt because 'that's the way it is here'. When you choose to follow others' style and approach, you will always react to your perceptions, because you're not living in the real world as your true authentic self. You have to break the mould and choose to respond to your own thoughts and feelings.

Your best version of you is not a carbon copy of some-one else. It can't be, because that's not you. Reflect on the leaders you have worked with and the moulds they set for others and recognise your own perceptions created by those moulds. What are they telling you to do? Who are they telling you to be? Other managers want you to be like them, because it makes them look good and puts them in control when you fit their mould. Leaders who fit the mould tell themselves that they have to do exactly what the boss says, as if the boss is some kind of demigod who controls them. But you control you; break the mould and be your-self, so you are in control of what happens to you.

Are you gonna try to make this work, or spend your days down in the dirt?

– THE STYLE COUNCIL

And then Covid came along

I worked with many leaders who broke the mould during the Covid-19 pandemic, making sure they supported their teams and took the time to build relationships not pressure.

But leaders who didn't break the mould during a global pandemic failed to do this. Instead, they reacted by:

➡ Sending an all-company email telling people to work harder from home

➡ Telling people they were at risk of redundancy via Zoom in front of the entire business

➡ Implementing a work-from-home dress code and asking people to show that they were wearing shoes during Microsoft Teams meetings

➡ Imposing daily check-ins on people at a time that only worked for the manager, showing no consideration for people's personal circumstances

➡ Simply sending all staff an email to tell them to get back to the office, nine to five, Monday to Friday, as soon as all social distancing restrictions were lifted

All of those things actually happened in the UK between March 2020 and July 2021. Seriously— they insisted on people wearing shoes in their home for a video call where people could only see their head and shoulders. I mean, get a grip, for fuck's sake!

If we had known what was coming in 2020 and asked every leader, 'If the world was sent into a global crisis tomorrow, would you want to support your people through it?', only the most selfish and narcissistic would say 'no'. Yet those things above actually happened; maybe you have even witnessed similar incidents yourself.

Leaders can end up getting shit from everyone and from everywhere. When you break the mould, you pick that shit up, bag it and bin it. It's how you go back to being you— for you and for those around you. The stress and pressure of being a leader doesn't go away; it just changes and intensifies. Breaking the mould enables you to choose a positive response to that stress and pressure, and it has an effective and inspirational impact on your leadership. It turns leaders away from spreading unhappiness and towards spreading happiness, choosing to never, ever, ever fit the mould!

**We all die. The goal isn't to live forever.
The goal is to create something that will.**

– CHUCK PALAHNIUK

Emotional intelligence will get you further in life than anything else

Just stop and think about how your thoughts and feelings work. No one ever says to themselves, 'Brain, now think this,' or, 'Heart, now make me feel like that.' Those thoughts and feelings will happen whether we ask them to or not. What you *can* tell yourself is how you want to respond and how you want to come across to other people. It is those thoughts and feelings that determine your natural reactions to the world around you.

To demonstrate this, consider how you respond when you ask yourself, 'What do I want other people to say about me?' You never answer with:

➡ I'm negative

➡ I'm unapproachable

➡ I'm a total prick

➡ I ignore people

➡ I don't listen

➡ I think I am always right

Yet that is how some leaders come across. This isn't because they are actually ignorant or difficult. It's because they are failing to control their emotions, which are triggered by a never-ending inbox of emails, relentless video calls, boring meetings and other people's negative attitudes and behaviours. Those emotions become your thoughts and feelings. When you get caught up in all that negativity, you are not being your true, authentic self. What we have to remember is that it's not the emails, the meetings or even the bad bosses that cause us problems. It's how we choose to respond, or not, to those things. Too often they turn into negative thoughts and feelings, which only takes us away from being who we really are.

Those emotions that invade our thoughts and feelings make us want the environment or other people to change, and we bemoan how hard it is to be a leader. You can't wait for other people to change; you have to start with you, break the mould and change you into the best version of you. Real leaders master their emotional triggers and choose to demonstrate attitudes and behaviours that inspire themselves and others, making positive choices to create an environment for empowerment where empathetic relationships thrive.

What I'm talking about here is emotional intelligence. It will get you further in life than anything else. Emotional intelligence is how you recognise, understand and choose a positive response to your emotions. It is how you choose your attitudes and behaviours to be your best version of you.

My years of studying and training others in coaching and developing emotional intelligence has shown me that it has two interconnected parts:

1. Your ability to recognise, understand and positively influence your own emotions

2. Your ability to recognise, understand and positively influence the emotions of others

Emotional intelligence is what will bring you more positive, productive days as a leader and make you happy when you go home. Without emotional intelligence, you can make your days worse no matter what ends up happening. With emotional intelligence, you can make your days better no matter what ends up happening. As the godfather of emotional intelligence, Daniel Goleman, has shown us, 'a leader's primal task is emotional leadership.'[1]

Emotional intelligence and breaking the mould go hand in hand. That's what this book will do for you: it will help you to manage your emotions, positively respond to your

---

1 Harvard Business Review's 10 Must Reads on Emotional Intelligence, 2015.

thoughts and feelings and create the impression that you want to create on others. To do all of that and break the mould, it always starts with you.

The single greatest power you have as a human being is your ability to choose how you respond to your thoughts and feelings.

All or nothing

The dangers of fitting the mould came into sharp focus for me when I was writing this book. If I want you to break the mould, then I have to make sure that the book role models that for you. You can't write a book called *Break the Mould* and then make it the same as all the other books out there! It has to be different; it has to focus on you, not on the 'solution'.

You're about to read the least leadership book-like leadership book that you'll ever come across. But it isn't really about leadership; it's about you. To demonstrate this point, I want to be totally transparent. I want you to understand two elements of the book that will help it to break the mould:

1. **Here comes the nice.**

Personal development is hard and it takes graft. You have to do it knowing that the (nice) change is coming. It needs you to commit to it and look inwardly for the answers, not expect someone else to simply give them to you. You've made the right choice to read this book, and when you get to the really good stuff it will be worth the wait. Too many leadership books give it all away at the start and then you're bored halfway through and left wondering what to do with the rest of it. Before you get to the 'how to' part, I will contextualise it for you and share stories to help you to make informed decisions for the role you will play in your own personal development. I will ask you more questions than I give you answers, and I ask you to bear with it because the time you invest in reading this book will absolutely pay off for you and will show you how to be your best version of you. If you want to skip straight to the 'how to' in Part Two, then go ahead and dive straight in, but it won't make as much sense without reading Part One first. Plus, you'll miss out on the ideas, stories, experiences and laughs that will make you really want to get the most out of Part Two. So I invite you to take the whole journey to learn more about you, understand more about the real context of leadership from true stories, and recognise how you can make positive choices.

2. **Music is power.**

It inspires me every day and fuels so much of what I do to help others. I want this book to repurpose your leadership, and music opens up a part of your heart and mind that enables you to do exactly that. You may already have noticed that the book uses a lot of music references and lyrics as inspirational quotes; this is a conscious choice I have made so that the book doesn't sound or feel like the 'same old, same old'. If I were to repeat the same old inspirational quotes from the same old people that everyone else uses, then I would be fitting the mould. I can't fill the book with exactly the same references that hundreds of other leadership books are full of, or you will forget what you learn about yourself and not be motivated to break the mould. So I am using music to help you to break the mould because music already does this for you. The songs you listened to in your childhood shape your identity. Music is already a memory aid for you and can take you back to a specific time in your life. Music is people-centric; it's not about theory and doing it in a particular way. The same song can mean a million different things to a million different people. And that's what the book gives you the licence to do – choose what it means to you and how you will make it part of your leadership. We can remember the lyrics to a song we first heard over 20 years ago, yet we don't always remember who we really are. This makes us fit the mould and lose sight of our best version of us. The way we remember music should be applied to how we remember our true authentic selves, helping us to choose how we behave based on that; you should create the soundtrack to your life. Use the lyrics throughout this book to create a playlist that you will remember forever.

Music is power.
Let it flow through your mind.

– RICHARD ASHCROFT

CHAPTER 1

WHY YOU'RE STILL READING LEADERSHIP BOOKS

As you're starting a brand new book, take this moment to ask yourself:

➡ Who are you?

➡ Why are you a leader?

➡ What do you want from being a leader?

➡ What do you expect from yourself as a leader?

➡ How does your leadership approach align with your personal values?

➡ What brings you joy in your job?

Before you turn the page, take a few minutes to think about your answers to those questions; maybe even write them down.

These questions kick off the *Break the Mould* workbook that is available from **www.italwaysstartswithyou.com,** so now might be time to invest in that if you haven't done so already.

When was the last time you were asked those questions, or asked yourself those questions, or explored yourself and your leadership and ensured you were clear on who you are and what you expect from yourself as a leader? That's what leads to you being able to make positive choices to break the mould.

You have to know where you want your choices to come from. It always starts with you.

Leadership is now more important than ever

… Said the first leadership book ever written.

… Said the best-selling leadership book of the last 10 years.

… Said every leadership book written in the last 30 years.

… Said every leadership training course ever written and delivered.

… Said every podcast, article, e-book and blog about leadership.

… Said everyone in response to the Covid-19 pandemic.

Let's not kid ourselves that leadership is only important now, in our time. It has always been very important. Let's also not kid ourselves that we've never fallen for the quick wins as we search for the answers to 'how to lead a team', the ubiquitous '10 things that effective managers do', or of course the books and training courses that guarantee to 'change the way you lead'.

There is no such thing as a quick win in leadership, and there is no guaranteed way to lead people – because people are people; all of us are different and need different things from our leaders. Leadership needs hard work, commitment and time and – most importantly – it needs you to break the mould.

Leadership has been tried, written about, talked about and learnt about for hundreds of years. You being a leader is your chance to write your own chapter in the continuing history of leadership. How many leadership training courses have you attended that were about what other people told

"Leadership needs hard work, commitment and time and — most importantly — it needs you to break the mould."

you to do or to be? How many leadership development programmes have you sat through that were not actually about the thing that makes all the difference in your leadership – YOU?

Supermodels

How many times have people tried to convince you that their approach to leadership was going to make you a better leader? They promised it would teach you what to say, how to act, or 'when to lead and when to manage'. However, we leave those experiences still no clearer on how to be the leader we want to be– or feel confident being it!

Many books and training courses tell us that their new supermodel of leadership will solve all our problems. We're told that the secret to our success lies in this new model of two As, three Bs and four Cs. We're told to fit the mould of what a perceived 'leadership guru' thinks we should be. In fact, we spend hours learning all this in the hope that it will make those we lead suddenly change and create a utopia for us because we can follow someone else's leadership model or style.

Then we finish the book, leave the training course and forget pretty much all of it. No supermodel of leadership helps us when we go back to work and are still faced with the boss who micromanages us and the same 'difficult conversations' that we find daunting and uncomfortable.

Leadership books and training have got themselves into a habit of regurgitating the same old stuff – leaving you feeling even more frustrated, hopeless or lost – and they can make you feel like giving up and sleepwalking into becoming an 'I'll just do what I've always done' kind of leader. That's because so much of it is rhetoric from the same script.

It's old-fashioned and outdated. Telling us that we should follow 'this approach' with this kind of person and use 'that strategy' for that kind of person. Getting us to focus our attention on others and creating an expectation that they should behave exactly as we want them to, all because we have started leading according to someone else's model or copying the example of other leaders and organisations. This approach to leadership results in managers saying things like, 'I need you to tell me how to get this person to...' or, 'How do I change my team?'

The mould for leadership books and training was set long ago: tell you lots of theory, give you other people's ideas, stick a 'sage on the stage' to tell you all about their own or other people's success stories. Spoiler alert: leadership is not about other people – it's about you! You can learn a strategy for every single personality type and it still won't work. You can't change or control another person – you can only change or control you.

Three of the biggest areas of leadership development are communication, giving feedback and time management, and we're told to adopt this technique or use this model. They're all great ideas and many of them come from years of intellectual research. But what many of them fail to do is start with you, asking what you want to happen and what you can do to make that happen. There's no magic wand or silver bullet with leadership models and styles.

Before you 'choose your weapon' for how to approach the situations you face, stop and consider these three areas:

➡ For your communication, ask yourself: what do I want my communication to achieve?

➡ For giving feedback, ask yourself: what is the positive change that my feedback will create?

➡ For time management, ask yourself: what will I make happen today?

Don't be who they tell you to be – be who you want to be – no one ever gets fired for being the best version of themselves.

Leadership inertia or leadership inspiration – it's your choice

Something that stands out from many forms of leadership is how often we're told to manage people and things. There is only one thing in the entire world that you should ever manage, and that's *you*. Never, ever think of yourself or introduce yourself as their manager – *no you are not*.

No one wakes up in the morning thinking, 'Yes! I get to go to work today and be managed!' People want to be empowered by their leader; they want to be inspired by the person who has responsibility for leading them and for making decisions that affect them and their work.

It's this insistence on managing people and things that creates leadership inertia for many organisations. We're told that we should have a 'Manager's Toolkit'. Toolkits are great if you're leading a car or a fridge! You're not; you're leading people. Is it any wonder that organisations are full of managers who get promoted to their level of incompetence? After all, the world is telling us to fit a mould and that we should learn to manage in this way or that way and that there is a formula for us to be successful as a manager. Often, that mould is even predetermined by the organisation you work for.

Meet the new boss. Same as the old boss.

– THE WHO

This expectation – overt or covert – to fit a mould is great if you lead a team that wants to do exactly what you tell them to do. But for many of us, the truth of leadership is that we end up leading a team of people who come to work wondering how they ended up working here... with us!

News flash: people don't always do what you tell them to do – they do what *they* tell themselves to do.

Stop looking for someone else to give you the answer or magic leadership formula, because it doesn't exist. Break the mould and focus on being you; many leaders ask me, 'What kind of leader should I be?' and my response is always, 'First understand what kind of person you are, and use that to guide what kind of leader you want to be.'

Don't look for a leadership guru; look for someone who will help you to learn more about yourself.

Leadership is about the choices you make. Every choice you make should be done with the aim of becoming your best version of you – you can't live up to something that you haven't chosen to be.

Follow your own path from here
So don't listen to what they say
Cause inside, you've a heart of gold
So don't let them take this away.

– DOVES

The never-ending story

Think about the leadership books you have read or training courses you have completed within, let's say, the last 10 years. I can guarantee that they will have been written by, be about or reference some or all of:

➡ Dan Pink

➡ Jack Welch

➡ Jim Collins

➡ Jim Kerr

➡ John Adair

➡ John Kotter

➡ Ken Blanchard

➡ Peter Drucker

➡ Simon Sinek

➡ Someone who worked at Google

➡ Steve Jobs

➡ Steve Peters

➡ Warren Buffett

I've read all their books and love them all – many of them are authors and thought leaders who have helped me massively. What none of them has given me, though, is advice on how to do it in the moment as a leader, how to choose positive responses to the world around me. They don't say how to break the mould and deal with the most important part of human leadership: what is going on inside my heart and mind.

We're too often told to only see leadership as senior figures with authority or a successful story. How many times are Peter Drucker and Warren Buffett or Jack Welch quoted in books? Seriously– read 100 leadership or business books and count how many times Jim Collins, Jim Kerr or Ken Blanchard are referenced!

That's not a criticism of those leaders or amazing authors. It's an observation that we're often told the same thing and given the same mould to fit into. That can make us feel like a failure because we're not a millionaire CEO or because our teams don't react positively when we go for the Steve Jobs 'your work is shit' feedback approach! The best thing I learnt about myself as a leader is that I'm not Steve Jobs and all the others; I'm me, and that's all I've got to work on. Start with you, the decent human being that you are, and learn how to be your best version of you.

Among the inspirational stories and anecdotes that those authors or leaders tell us are many things that are actually outside of our control. They tell me to get rid of underper-formers, but very few leaders actually have that autonomy. They tell me to focus on earning lots of profit and expand-ing the business, but very few leaders are actually leaders of their organisation; they lead teams within the company. For every one CEO, there are tens or hundreds of other leaders within the same organisation. They tell me inspira-tional stories of other people's achievements, which gives me that warm fuzzy feeling inside and makes me want to take on the world. However, knowing what a US Air Force pilot or brain surgeon has done doesn't help me when I've got to have another conversation with angry Rita or nega-tive Sue and underperforming Bob too. It definitely doesn't help me when my micromanaging boss insists that I join another MS Teams call for the fifteenth time today!

Whether you're a CEO, a small business owner, a middle manager of 20 years or an aspiring leader, this book will help you because it's about you and shows you how to break the mould. That's what helps you in the moment: it always starts with you.

I'm not going to overwhelm you with psychology or scientific research that you don't really understand or can't translate to your job. The research for this book has been done in the best place– the real world– and comes from my own 20 years of leadership experience and from working with thousands of different people in hundreds of different organisations. I'm definitely not writing an academic tome for people to celebrate and reference for years to come – it's about you. Many leadership books or training courses are not written for you; they're written about famous success stories to help a publisher sell more books. Worse still, they are based on an employer's vision of what management is, and they result in leaders trying to fit the mould and becoming more and more frustrated because so-and-so's leadership style doesn't seem to work for them or their team.

Consider the leadership books that you've read and the training you've completed: how many of them actually asked you, 'Who do you want to be? What is your best version of you?' That's what we will focus on together, because that is the leader you want to be – you, not someone's else's version of a leader or someone else's solution.

Let's not worry about what others do, say or tell us to do. Let's focus on and work on you and let's break the mould.

You gotta be who you want to be in this life – don't be who they tell you to be.

– MADONNA

Leaders are people too

Let's not lose sight of the fact that leaders are human beings first. They have thoughts and feelings like everyone else. When we chase leadership success based on what others did or what they tell us to do, we stop looking for ourselves and instead waste time searching for the right 'style' or end up trying to be something we're not.

This not only blocks your career, but also leads to stress, being overwhelmed, a negative internal narrative, doubting your own abilities and even imposter syndrome. Your personal brand becomes confusing and convoluted when you start trying to be someone else's version of a leader or look for a leadership style to adopt. Don't look for a leadership style – look for you, because it always starts with you.

**And when you're knocked on your back
and your life's a flop
And when you're down on the bottom
there's nothing else
But to shout to the top (shout)
We're gonna shout to the top (shout).**

– THE STYLE COUNCIL

Before we move on, let's get something straight. A leader must:

➡ Achieve results

➡ Collaborate

➡ Communicate well

➡ Create the strategy

➡ Encourage and develop others

➡ Get shit done

➡ Innovate

➡ Make decisions

➡ Set the vision

However, first a leader must be enthused to lead themselves and others and focus on achieving positive influence. We need to drop the desire to increase a leader's IQ or force them to upskill in certain areas, like time management (you can't manage time – good luck trying), and give leaders the opportunity to lead as their true, authentic selves. That makes it possible to do all the things a leader must do, while creating an open and harmonious environment in which people can think for themselves and do their best work. I have worked with all manner of organisations– from large corporations to the NHS, from housing associations to digital start-ups, from family-run businesses to Premier League football clubs– and it's always the same challenges. People are people.

Search online for 'why leadership development pro-grammes fail' and you'll find literally millions of results. The biggest failures that I've witnessed first-hand were due to the focus being put on making people fit into a mould, tell-ing them 'how to be a manager'. We see a challenge in an organisation and quickly prescribe how to manage our way out of it. This is the mould that we're trying to make leaders fit into: 'there is a problem, so manage your way out of it'. People are being trained every day to better manage:

➡ Their relationships

➡ Their time

➡ Giving feedback

➡ Their communication

➡ Change

Instead of telling leaders how to manage these things, let's engage with you and ask:

➡ What do you want from your relationships as a leader?

➡ What does a great day look like for you?

➡ What positive change do you want to help others achieve with your feedback?

➡ How do you want to come across in your communication?

➡ Why is change important?

There is a lack of focus on the individual in the typical approach to leadership development; everyone is expected to just fit the same mould, like robots. Too often it's like,

'Here's a load of content and theory, now go off and do exactly what everyone else does with it'. Or, even worse, it's slanted towards the organisation's agenda or standards, which are often set by people who have never even led a team or organisation before. We need to be making it easier for leaders by giving you the time and space to develop you. Develop your best version of you. No amount of 'managing things' will get you to that place. When you've developed that, having conversations, creating strategies, solving problems, everything else becomes much easier.

It's easy to choose 'time management' because leaders have got too much work to do or to choose 'leading change' because the organisation is constantly changing things. Neither is particularly helpful to leaders unless they have the emotional competence to implement new habits, change their behaviours, see things from a different perspective and have the conversations that matter. All of that is achieved by starting with you. You can't control time or change – the only thing that you are always 100% in control of is how you choose to respond to your thoughts and feelings. When you recognise that and choose your response, then you are the leader who stands up for what you believe in, not someone who tells people off for wearing the wrong shoes!

There is no secret to leadership. The real secret is to discover you. To break the mould. To trust your commitment. Trust your integrity. To stick to your principles. After all, if you do what you believe in, then others will believe in you. It Always Starts With You.

So what?

➡ Leadership is not about other people's success or supermodels; it's about you.

➡ People don't always do what you tell them to do – they do what they want to do.

➡ What people really want from you as a leader is your true, authentic self.

➡ Leaders are people too – getting the title 'manager' doesn't stop you being a human being.

➡ There are lots of leadership experts out there, but you need to be the expert on you.

➡ Inertia or inspiration as a leader? It's your choice.

Get enthused

➡ What do you want to get from reading this book?

➡ What do you want to learn about yourself from reading this book?

➡ What is the best version of you as a leader that you want to be?

➡ What do you want to change about how you lead others?

➡ How are other people's realities trumping yours?

➡ What have you already learnt about being a leader that helps you?

CHAPTER 2

THE REALITIES OF LEADERSHIP

**Leadership is built on loyalty,
trust and communication.**

– SIR ALEX FERGUSON

Leadership is not always what you expect it to be. When I took on my first leadership role, I never expected that I would be set off on the journey that I have had as a leader or have the experiences that I have had. This is also the case for so many other leaders. One such leader who stands out for me is Jo, who was a retail store manager for a well-known fashion brand.

I worked with Jo as part of the team development that I facilitated with her and her store teams based at two of the UK's biggest shopping centres. Jo was asked to take on the responsibility for leading two flagship stores and is one of the most positive, committed and resilient leaders I have ever worked with, yet the expectations placed upon her and her teams, and the reality of leadership in that organisation, provided a stark contrast to what she was told her role would be. Jo eloquently summed this up by telling me:

I was told that being a leader would mean a chance to inspire others. To develop and progress. I was sold the dream. The reality is that I spend my days dealing with piss, shit and tampons.

They don't put that on your job description!

With that in mind, and before we get stuck in to how you can break the mould, let's remind ourselves of the realities of leadership. I am going to share with you some real stories about leaders I have worked with, the moulds I was expected to fit into and the life lessons I learnt as a leader.

The realities of leadership are why looking for someone else's solution or leadership style is not the answer to you being your best version of you. You are the answer.

What is the greater risk: changing or staying the same?

– ADAM KARA

I got sick of working for dickheads

Attendee at networking event: 'So, Tim, what made you quit your job and set up Enthuse?'

Me: 'I got sick of working for dickheads.'

While my response to the question might seem facetious or unprofessional, I say it this way because it's the truth. If you've ever worked for a dickhead, you know where I'm coming from.

Google's online dictionary definition of dickhead: 'a stupid, irritating or ridiculous person'.[2]

---

2   https://www.google.com/search?q=dickhead+definition

Below are some of the worst things the dickheads I worked with said or did. I hope you haven't had to deal with any of this shit but, given the sheer volume of dickhead managers out there, you might be able to relate:

➡ 'When I want your opinion, little girl, I will ask for it.' This particular dickhead was the CEO of a business who publicly claimed to empower young women! His words to the only female member of the executive board were totally unacceptable.

➡ 'Have you even got a brain, Tim?' I was an 18-year-old in my first job when my boss asked me this. In the middle of the office. In front of everyone else. Imagine if I fitted into that mould, thinking it was OK to patronise and embarrass a young, inexperienced member of the team just because they made a mistake…

➡ 'I work in HR because I don't like people.' This dickhead was an egotistical, uninterested HR manager who publicly hated everyone and really loved himself. I went against my own instincts and followed his instructions for how to handle the dismissal of a young woman – who duly punched me in the face. It was definitely a case of shooting the messenger but, to be honest, I don't blame her.

➡ 'Don't put depression on your return-to-work form. Other people will see it, and you don't want people knowing that you've got mental health problems.' This was said to me by a head of HR when I shared that I had been diagnosed with anxiety and depression. Imagine telling someone to lie about their mental health after they'd opened up to you about it... No wonder there's still so much stigma around it and people think they have to fit the mould of not talking about their mental health!

➡ 'I don't pay you to think.' This classic is one of my favourite things ever said to me by Incompetent Ian (more of him later). By this time in my leadership career, I'd started to break the mould, which meant I had started to think. So I replied with, 'What do you pay me for, then?' Ian didn't get it!

Trying to get some explanation here about the way people are.

– DAVID GRAY

While this behaviour was 100% unacceptable, I don't blame those people for their dickhead behaviour, judge them for it or hold it against them; some of them, deep down, are decent human beings. They were simply products of their environment, fitting the mould they perceived they had to fit. They had lost sight of their true, authentic selves without even realising it and had never even considered breaking the mould, let alone realised how important it is. It's actually much easier to be a dickhead than it is to be your best version of you.

The dickheads are the managers who blindly fit the mould. They try too hard to be the 'best version of themselves' that someone else imposes on them. They seek to fit in and take the path of least resistance. All of them started out alright... then they let their environment, other people and the company culture shape them, and they turned into Frankenstein's monster. Even Incompetent Ian didn't intend to piss people off!

And the dickheads are all ages.

– SAM FENDER

"Don't choose to be another dickhead — choose to break the mould and be your best version of you."

Being a dickhead is a way to stay in your comfort zone, where you do what you've always done. Your best version of you is outside of your comfort zone; you have to consciously choose to be it and choose to deliberately break the mould. So much of that dickhead behaviour comes from how those people were taught to be leaders. They were taught to expect others to do exactly as they tell them and to be like them. When that doesn't happen, they don't know how to choose a positive response to their thoughts and feelings, so they go into reactive mode and demonstrate dickhead behaviour.

As I started to become more aware of the dickhead behaviour, it made me realise that I had to make a choice: choose whether to continue trying to navigate and appease the dickheads, or choose to be my best version of me.

Don't choose to be another dickhead – choose to break the mould and be your best version of you.

These are the moulds that those particular dickheads were trying to fit into and how they could have broken those moulds:

DICKHEAD	THE MOULD THEY FIT	BREAK THE MOULD BY
Inappropriate CEO	They must be in charge and have the power. The only thing that matters is profit and serving the investors.	Listening to people and allowing the brilliant people that you employ to get on with their jobs.
Patronising boss	These youngsters are nothing but trouble. Speak to them like an angry parent and show them that you are the boss.	Setting clear expectations. Engaging with the 18-year-old as you would have liked someone to engage with you when you started your first full-time job.
HR manager with no personality	Show people that HR isn't pink and fluffy and that we have authority.	Being a decent human being and seeing that HR actually is all about people.
Head of HR with no self-awareness	Don't talk about mental health; just help people to cover it up.	Asking the person with depression what *they* would like to put on *their* return-to-work form and what support they need.
Incompetent Ian	People should do as they are told and not think for themselves, because that's what I do.	Encouraging people to think for themselves and asking them for their ideas.

Trust your commitment. Trust your integrity. Stick to your principles.

– NOVA FERGUSON

All those moulds that the dickheads were trying to fit into came from their own thoughts and feelings. No one told them to belittle their peers, to patronise office juniors, to tell people that they didn't care, that they had no compassion or that they were supposed to hold people back. They chose those moulds for themselves because they couldn't choose a positive response to the thoughts and feelings brought on by their roles and circumstances.

Look at how they could have broken the mould – it's hardly ground-breaking stuff! It just takes a positive choice, and everyone is capable of it. Breaking the mould isn't just your very own personal dickhead prevention insurance policy; it also makes sure that you have the level of awareness required to be a leader– awareness of yourself and how you impact on others. It gives you the consistent awareness that leadership is not about what you do or the results you get; it's about your attitudes and behaviours.

Here are two real leaders I witnessed at first hand who either lost that awareness or never had it to start with…

All that for a fucking Calippo!

Picture the scene: you're at work, sitting in a meeting that isn't exactly getting you excited. It's a glorious summer day outside; the sun is shining, and it's very hot. It's the kind of day where the last place you want to be is sitting inside a poorly air-conditioned room, distracted by your thoughts of where else you'd like to be and what else you could be doing.

Then the boredom is punctuated by the sight and sound of an ice cream van approaching down the road. Its chimes are playing, and it takes you back to your childhood in your mind; all you can now think about is how much you want an ice cream – a proper ice cream from a proper ice cream van. Your attention is now completely gone from the meeting around you and you start to stare intently at the ice cream van, allowing yourself to think, 'Imagine if it pulls into the car park and I can get out of here.' Then you see that the van is indicating your way and it just might happen. It *is* happening. It's turning into your office car park. You can't hide your excitement now, and your bum is slowly coming off the chair as you interrupt the meeting, pointing out of the window and exclaiming, 'There's an ice cream van here!' like you did when you were a kid. No one else in the meeting seems as excited as you – maybe they are actually interested in this God-awful meeting – and one of them plainly says, 'Oh, yeah – Garry said he'd arranged for an ice cream van to come today. It's free.'

'Free ice cream? Why is no one else as excited as me?' you think, and that's it – you're off. Everyone accepts that it's a good time to take a break, and you head outside to get a 99. When you are outside, there is already a long queue and you join the back of it, quite happy that it might take a while to get served as it means more time outside rather than losing more of your life to a boring meeting.

You're happily enjoying being outside in the sunshine, making small talk with your colleagues, when the peace is abruptly punctured by someone behind you loudly exclaiming, 'For fuck's sake! How long is this queue?' You turn to see an IT manager moving to either side of the queue of people, lifting his head and standing on his tiptoes to see the front. He's clearly agitated, and most people are now turning to look at him.

'Jesus. What is the point of giving us free ice cream if it takes us ages to get it?' he continues, still swaying around and not making eye contact with anyone, still audibly sharing his displeasure. 'I've got loads to do. This isn't fair. Why didn't they tell us an ice cream van was coming? I could have got outside first.' He is now trying to engage with the people at the back of the queue, who look at each other awkwardly, considering whether to respond to him. It is one of those classic moments at work where everyone knows that what he is saying is wrong and that he should just calm down and either join the queue or go back inside but no one wants to be *that* person who confronts him. You all just want to enjoy the sunshine and get a free ice cream without having an argument with an angry bloke from IT.

'I've got too much to do to stand here queuing. I'm supposed to be in a meeting.' With that, he storms past you and towards the front of the queue.

Everyone's conversation around you turns to the subject of his behaviour. Some people are laughing, others are angry about it, and some start imitating him. A few minutes later, he walks back past the queue with a Calippo ice lolly in his hand which he has somehow managed to acquire either through pushing in or by getting someone at the front of the queue to get it for him.

Now everyone in the queue shows their real frustration and starts to criticise the IT manager. This is Britain on a hot summer's day; you *do not* queue jump here! One person calls him a dickhead, while someone else suggests that IT gets special privileges, and someone you're standing with says, 'I've got a meeting with him in a bit– can't wait for that!' You're still in shock at what has just happened. In the space of 10 minutes, you've gone from being sat in a boring meeting to childlike free-ice-cream euphoria to now being surrounded by an angry mob.

You are still just happy to be out of your boring meeting and in the sunshine. You let out a sigh and say, 'Wow. All that for a fucking Calippo!'

You are what you do, so ask yourself whenever you're doing something: is this reflective of the person that I want to be?

– RYAN HOLIDAY

The parable of the oversized cheque

When I worked at a national sales organisation, I would attend the annual sales conference. The first time I was there, the Sales Manager of the Year award was given to the same person who had won it for the previous two years. As they collected their oversized cheque for a £1,000 bonus, we all dutifully applauded and I turned to my colleague next to me and said, 'Three years running? He must be good at what he does.'

Their reply was not what I expected. 'He's a massive twat. No one can stand him. The reason he wins this award every year is because all his staff leave so he has to be the one doing all the selling!'

In his moment of glory, this particular leader might not have cared what others thought of him and, for the day of the sales conference, he could bask in his success and laud it over his peers. But once he's banked the cheque and spent the £1,000, what he's left with is himself (and a hangover!) and his thoughts and feelings as he returns to an empty, soulless workplace where the people he works with don't actually care that he's £1,000 richer, because he will still behave and treat them in the same way.

**Lead by what is important to you,
not by what you do.**

You can win all the £1,000 cheques you want; if you can't deal with people, you will always be known as a massive twat, and no one will ever want to do anything for you.

It's not about what you know; it's about the choices you make.

You are not your thoughts; you are your choices

While the dickheads, the angry IT manager and the 'massive twat' may be extreme examples, they are stark reminders of the realities of leadership. I am not sharing these examples to shock you or frighten you. I want them to make you think about what you really want and how important it is to navigate the real world of leadership guided not by your workload or remuneration but by you, your values and how you really want to behave.

That experience at the ice cream van will never leave me (I was the one in the boring meeting, *not* the angry IT manager!); nor will the experience of over 500 people applauding a 'massive twat' holding aloft an oversized novelty cheque. They are perfect examples of the realities of what it can be like as a leader, for both the leader themselves and those around them.

A reality of leadership that we need to be aware of is that people genuinely don't care about how many sales targets you can hit or how many IT projects you can deliver on time and on budget. They might care about it for a moment in time– and maybe even celebrate your results with you for a finite period– but I've never met anyone who can tell me about the specific business results that leaders they have worked with have achieved. What they *can* tell me about is the attitudes those leaders had, how those leaders behaved, the reputation they had and the impact they had on other people. What people really care about is you – your values, your attitudes and your behaviours. They remember the choices you make to be a confident and happy leader as your best version of you. A manager who outperforms their team does not make a good leader.

Stop and raise your awareness now by asking yourself:

➡ What are the attitudes and behaviours that you want to be known for?

➡ How do you want to come across as a leader?

➡ What impact do you want to have on others?

➡ What do you want other people to say about you?

If any of those leaders whose example I have shared with you had stopped to ask themselves those questions, there is no way they would then have made sexist comments or belittled other people or got apoplectic in a queue for free ice cream or stood on stage taking the credit for others' hard work. It always starts with you, and the more awareness you have of yourself and how you want to behave, the more you can achieve positive realities in your leadership.

No one is perfect. I have my own life lesson to share with you where I misinterpreted the reality of my own leadership and had to raise my awareness of the choices I could make.

A life lesson: 'I'm sick of talking to the back of your head.'

I heard those words not long after I had been promoted to lead the team I was part of. I thought I knew it all. I had worked hard and I was one of the best performers in the team, with exceptional technical knowledge of the job. I was well respected by the bosses, and this was my time to show everyone that I was the up-and-coming leader in this business. I even bought a new suit! All that youthful enthusiasm and (misplaced) confidence doesn't help you if you don't have any awareness of what's really going on.

One of the habits I had picked up as the new boss in the new suit was that I could keep typing away and sending emails and generally doing work while my team were talking to me. This was done in all innocence because my thoughts told me I was being effective and efficient: 'Look at me, I can do my work and have a conversation at the same time' was how it looked in my head. How wrong was I?

One member of the team, Sarah, had had enough of it. The next time I did it to her, she stopped speaking, let out an audible sigh and said, loudly enough for others to hear, 'I am sick of talking to the back of your head, Tim.'

It forced me to turn and face her. Luckily for me, Sarah's cutting feedback switched on my awareness and, as her words sent shivers down my spine, I turned and noticed that many of the other team members had heard her and were either nervously watching for my reaction or were trying to hide their nervous laughter; Sarah had finally said what they all wanted to say to me. In that moment, I chose to engage with Sarah and give her my full attention, but it shouldn't have needed her to tell me to do that!

I later asked another member of the team, with whom I had a strong relationship, what he thought of what Sarah had said to me. He told me in no uncertain terms that she had done everyone a favour. He told me that people had been talking about me being ignorant and sharing with each other how much it pissed them off. This was turning their impression of me from someone they worked well with to someone who didn't care and wasn't interested in them.

My thoughts were telling me I was really good at my job and that multitasking by completing my work at the same time as telling my team what to do was a good thing. However, my team's thoughts were that I was an ignorant prick!

**It's easy living in a bubble
And no complication or trouble
But it's hard to have responsibility.**

– THE BLUETONES

What life lesson are you waiting for to show you the reality of your leadership for you and those around you? My thoughts told me that my team would trust me because I could do what they did and that I could multitask– when, in reality, that was the last thing they wanted from me. One of the leadership mistakes I had fallen foul of when making my team talk to the back of my head was believing that my thoughts and feelings were right; believing them when they were telling me to be in control of the work and the outputs and that the way to do that would be to do the work myself. I believed I needed to 'get my hands dirty' and project an impression of me that I always knew best and always knew what to do.

A reality of leadership is this:

WHAT'S IN YOUR CONTROL	WHAT'S NOT IN YOUR CONTROL
Your attitudes and behaviour	Everything else

Can you see the good things in your life?
See what's really happening and why?

– PAUL WELLER

What mould are you expected to fit?

We'd love the mould that we're expected to fit into to be the kind that is portrayed externally with an employer brand and at job interviews. You know the type of thing: values, opportunities, progression and the dream that gets sold to you. The reality is that the mould you are expected to fit is rarely the one that's on your job description. Like the mould where you have to manage someone who applied for your job and now blames you for not getting it. Or the mould where half your team hates you because you replaced the old boss they all liked because she made it really easy for them and was everyone's best mate.

'We need you to come in and sort them out, Tim.' That was the message I was given when I was offered the job as senior leader at a well-known large organisation. This made me think they really wanted me; it gave me confidence that I could go in and make a difference and that I was the saviour they had been waiting for to 'sort them out'. What they really meant was that they needed someone to do the dirty work for them. In reality, my boss had convinced his boss that they were too busy to sort out the behaviour and performance problems in their team. Instead, they had created a new leadership role, someone they would manipulate and simply tell to address the ongoing issues, taking the pressure off them as they could turn to their bosses and tell them that 'Tim is sorting that out'. I was expected to do all of that while working in a blame culture where collaboration was a buzzword that people didn't actually understand, never mind practise.

It was a classic example of 'here's your job title and job description. And here's what we *really* want you to do'. The mould you're expected to fit into is never described on the job advert.

This role led to nothing but stress and disappointment for me. I had strained relationships with some members of the team and felt like I was trapped in a vicious circle. The stress and frustrations I experienced can be traced back to the mould that I was expected to fit into.

**Ignore the people who think
it's weird to be weird.**

– GAVIN OATTES

In every team and in every organisation, there is a mould which we're expected to fit. For some, that is a very positive mould– it is empowering, a place where they can be themselves– and that determines their successful results. Unfortunately, for a lot of us that is not the reality, and we either end up fitting the mould expected of us, sacrificing ourselves and allowing our job to define us, or we keep on searching and searching for the mould that does fit us. There is a reason why the recruitment business is a multi-billion-dollar global industry!

Gig economy, my arse! 'The Great Resignation' is being caused by people changing jobs more often because they are trying to escape the mould that is being cast for them.

Even this book is expected to fit a certain mould: a mould that makes it easy for people to label it and to fit it into a specific format and category, because that's what other people do. Well, I'm not doing that! I will write the book in a way that I believe in, so I am proud of it. Why should anyone put something out into the world that other people have told them to do? The most important thing for me about writing this book is that I can look into the eyes of my wife and kids and tell them that I wrote in a way that represents me and what I believe in, not the way that everyone else told me to. That's the only way to take true accountability for what you do; if I follow the mould of all other leadership books, I will have the excuse to blame that mould if it isn't a success, but what I will be left with will be the nagging thought 'Why didn't I do it in the way I wanted to?', which will beat me up for the rest of my life.

And it's the same with your leadership: you have to choose to do it your way. A way that makes you sleep well at night and will give you the ability to look back on your career in later life and say that you did things in the way you believed was right, not the way everyone else told you to.

**Come to a point in my life
where I've been searching.
Searching for the old days.
Where I could be myself.
Dreams don't die, they get old.**

– THE RECORD COMPANY

Breaking the mould isn't about being a rebel or just being different for the sake of it. It's about getting to know the true, authentic you and leading with that. Accepting the realities of leadership and choosing a positive response. Some of the classic moulds that you're expected to fit into that I have seen in many organisations include:

➡ Don't take personal development seriously; 'just do what you've always done.'

➡ Be afraid of the senior leaders/owners of the business and never challenge their behaviour or their ideas— even though they are negative and ineffective, and everyone knows it.

➡ Ignore the same old problems and attitudes of others, because we're making a profit.

➡ 'That's just the way it is here; you'll get used to it'– which roughly translates into 'Don't even think about trying to change anything; we're all comfortable here and don't want you to make us look bad.'

➡ Try to solve problems with updated policies instead of actually talking openly about them and finding a positive solution. Just send an all-company email and stick up some laminated signs – that will do the trick.

➡ Be patient for things to change while your incompetent boss becomes more and more submissive to the dictatorial CEO.

➡ Control your team and everything they do, because if your boss needs something from you urgently, then they expect you to sort it for them immediately.

➡ 'Just get on with it' (or the less articulate 'just fucking do it'), and don't expect any support or recognition for what you do.

A lot of the dickheads would look at the above and say that you're too soft if you can't cope with those things and that 'you're here to do a job, not to make friends'. That's why they are constantly recruiting to replace people who leave them. When said dickheads are asked about their work, the most imaginative answers they can come up with are things like, 'Same old, same old. Lots going on,' or a shrug of the shoulders accompanied by, 'It's alright'. If you want to spend 40+ years of your life doing a job that is just 'alright' and feels like the 'same old, same old', then put down this book and crack on with fitting the moulds that are made for you by other people.

While you can't control the mould you are expected to fit or the realities of leadership, you are always 100% in control of how you choose to respond to your thoughts and feelings and how you can break the mould.

Let's do a quick check-in to recognise your own perceptions. Answer the following questions honestly:

➡ What mould are you expected to fit into where you work?

➡ What mould are you expecting your team to fit into?

➡ What moulds are you in danger of upholding?

➡ What moulds have you created in your head for yourself to fit into?

➡ What moulds are you being led into?

You don't have to be that good. As long as you've got something about you, you'll go a long way.

— LIAM GALLAGHER

Don't rely on what you already know; rely on what you are yet to learn

The absolute reality of leadership is that you have to make your choices based on being a decent human being. You have to be able to choose a positive response to your thoughts and feelings. The realities of leadership are:

➡ It always starts with you.

➡ You choose how you behave.

➡ You need to be clear on your values and who you really are.

➡ The one and only thing that you are truly accountable for is living up to what you stand for… Every. Single. Day.

➡ Your reputation walks through the door before you do.

➡ Integrity beats ego every time.

➡ You have to be prepared and motivated to have real, two-way conversations every day.

➡ You have to only focus on what is within your control.

➡ You need to build trust before you build results.

➡ You are only as strong as the relationships you build.

➡ Self-awareness is the only superpower any human being can have.

➡ If you want people to give a shit about what they do, you first have to show them that you give a shit about them.

➡ Your thoughts and feelings are not always reality.

➡ The real gift of leadership is helping others to learn more about themselves.

A simple way to break the mould is to do something as a result of reading this book. There's no point reading it and learning from it if you do nothing with it. Think about the conversations you can have with your team. The different positive choices you can make. You fit the mould by attending the training course and reading books and then going back to what you've always done. Break the mould by doing something about it!

The past was yours but the future's mine.

– THE STONE ROSES

Managing versus leading

While the realities of leadership might make us question why we'd want to be a leader in the first place, let's remember the positives. For all the dickheads, ice cream queue aggravators and massive twats with big cheques, let's not forget the inspirational leaders. There's Zoe Sinclair, Martin Hesketh, Rob Johnson, Nova Ferguson, Aimee Bateman, Julia Darvill, Danny Seals, Karene Lamond, Lisa Gritton, Loiza Tallon and Jo Wright, to name but a few. Those names probably mean absolutely nothing to you, but they mean everything to me. Think of your own inspirational leaders and what they did for you. How they helped you to navigate the realities of leadership. The impact they had on you. Get in touch with them, thank them and ask them questions to understand more about how they break the mould.

When we remember the realities of leadership, it hammers home how important it is to break the mould. To be your true, authentic self – your best version of you. What's the other choice? Try to fit the mould that is already filled up with everyone else? There's much more room for you in your own mould. That's where people want you to be. They don't want you to be their 'manager'; they want you to lead them and inspire them – whoever you are, whatever you do, and wherever you do it.

Throughout this book, I use the term 'leaders' and not 'managers'. I choose to always say 'leader' because the reality is that's what people want (don't worry— this isn't a boring waffle about managers versus leaders; there are plenty of those elsewhere!). Yes, organisations need managers; of course they do. But what the people, the humans within those organisations, need is for you to be a leader. A leader who sees the reality of their situation and who leads them as your true, authentic self.

Some people say, 'I'm not a leader.' Then they justify it by downplaying their role in the business. They say, 'I'm just a shift manager, mate,' or, 'I manage a load of hairy-arse blokes. I'm not a leader,' or my favourite line ever, 'I'm not a leader— that's way above my pay grade'. It's got nothing to do with your job title, who you lead or what your pay grade is. We are all leaders, because we all lead at least one person on this earth: ourselves.

Trying to be someone's manager makes you feel under pressure, like you have to manage everything. When someone fucks up, you blame yourself and think that you have to manage your way out of it. It's like we think that leadership is reserved for senior leaders only, or the 'C Suite'. Some organisations even call only one team 'the leadership team'. Corporate bullshit, right there! Once you get the title 'manager', switch your internal focus to 'leader'. Whether you are leading a team of one or 100, you have to choose to break the mould to become the leader you want to be. You don't have to walk around saying, 'I am a leader,' or buy a new suit like I did! You have to say it to yourself first and then behave in the way you expect a leader to behave.

Another reality of leadership is this:

WHAT NEEDS MANAGING	WHAT NEEDS LEADING
• Systems	• You
• Processes	• Other people
• Projects	
• Budgets	
• Operational strategy	
• Tasks	

When you break the mould and choose to be a leader, the reality is that it is the greatest job on earth. You're given the opportunity to positively influence people's lives. You help them to learn more about themselves, to have a good day at work, and to believe in themselves. That's worth more than any salary or job title, and that's what people remember you for. No one will mention how much money you earned at your leaving do!

People would survive without organisations – indeed, they did for millions of years. But organisations can't survive without people. The reality is that organisations need to stop asking, 'What results will our leaders be responsible for?' and start asking, 'What impact on our people will our leaders be responsible for?' Don't wait for that to happen. You have to start with you and break the mould to make your own reality of leadership a positive experience for you and those around you.

The more you learn about yourself, the more you know who you want to be.

Don't forget to grab your *Break the Mould* workbook from **www.italwaysstartswithyou.com** to make your realities of leadership positive for you and those around you.

So what?

➡ You are not your thoughts; you are your choices.

➡ There are loads of dickheads out there – you have to choose not to be one.

➡ Your job title and job description don't define you. You are not your job; you are you.

➡ There's always a mould that you're expected to fit into – you have to break it.

➡ The absolute reality of leadership is that you have to make your choices based on being a decent human being.

➡ The realities of leadership are not what others tell you they are.

Get enthused

➡ What life lessons have you already learnt about leadership?

➡ What are the moulds that you're expected to fit into?

➡ What will you do to break those moulds?

➡ How will you make sure that you are not one of the dickheads?

➡ What are you yet to learn about leadership?

➡ How will you make leadership the greatest job on earth for you?

CHAPTER 3

IT ALWAYS STARTS WITH YOU

Caught up in this life

Of who we become

No time for thinking twice

If only someone said

This life ain't easy

But it's the one that we all got.

– STEREOPHONICS

Start me up

Whatever you want from being a leader, it always starts with you. You must always sort your own shit out first before you can start to lead others.

If you want to break the mould, then it always starts with you. If you want to be happy as a leader, then it always starts with you. If you want to be successful and get promoted, then it always starts with you. If you want to build relationships with your team and inspire people, then it always starts with you.

Conversely, if you want to be miserable as a leader, then it always starts with you. If you want to piss people off, then it always starts with you. If you want to become disenchanted with your work and your team, then it always starts with you. If you want to fit the mould that others set for you, then it always starts with you.

You spend more time at work than anywhere else. Your experience as a leader and how you feel at work is all within your control – because it always starts with you.

As long as you think the problem is out there, that very thought is the problem.

– STEPHEN COVEY

What has breaking the mould got to do with leadership?

Some leaders spend their entire careers trying and failing to master a version of leadership that is predetermined by someone else. Then they retire. You are not going to do that. The only thing you need to master is being you. People are naturally attracted to authenticity, and starting with you will take you back to your true, authentic self. By spending your time and energy mastering being you, you can stand up to the pressure from your boss and the organisation. You can lead a team that wants to be led by you, and move away from negative problems to positive solutions. When things go wrong, you're able to own your mistakes and ask, 'How do we make it better?' and, 'What will we learn from this?' You can stop being a busy fool and just be you. There's no need to have a 'work version of you' – just your best version of you. Whoever and wherever you are.

**You need to be yourself
You can't be no one else.**

– OASIS

The easy route for leaders is to imitate what they see around them and try to shape themselves to the mould. This is the habit that we adopt from a very early age and is part of our earliest experience of the world, so we expect leadership to be the same. Consider the baby who learns to walk by copying their parents and siblings, or the first words we speak, which come from others telling us how to say them. We go to school and our teachers tell us to learn by copying how and what they write, or show us in a textbook. These formative experiences create a perception in our minds that 'being different' is a threat and should be avoided. We should fit the mould that other people and our environment create for us. We have it built into us to learn how to behave by copying others and reacting to our environment. We're even encouraged to do that by the organisation we work for ('here's our values and behaviour framework – follow them').

I've lost count of how many times leaders have said things to me like, 'I behave differently at work than I do at home'… Why? Being a dickhead at work isn't OK just because you think you're not being a dickhead at home – you at work should be the same as you at home.

That's why starting with you is so important; it's how you break the mould. You can't take accountability while you're doing what everyone else is doing. You will never be truly happy and successful as a leader while you're trying to copy everyone else. Breaking the mould starts with you and empowers you to create your own perspective on how you

"I want you to start your days with you and ask yourself, 'What will I make happen today?' and, 'What impact will I have on others today?'"

should behave and build your relationships. Leaders who break the mould:

→ Are their authentic selves

→ Have the conversations that matter

→ Build positive relationships

→ Love their jobs

→ Find purpose in their work

→ See things from others' points of view

→ Respond well to stress and handle feeling over-whelmed in a positive way

→ Are happy

I want you to no longer start your days with a to-do list or a calendar full of meetings and calls that fill you with dread and stress. I want you to start your days with you and ask yourself, 'What will I make happen today?' and, 'What impact will I have on others today?'

The last thing you should ever want to be is just like everyone else.

People who try to master leadership end up blaming others for their mistakes, or become self-critical and allow results to ruin relationships. When you master being you, you have intrinsic motivation to keep rising to the challenge and to remain positive without feeling like you're going to get found out as a leader. When you get found out being you, then all people find is a decent human being.

You change the world by being yourself.

– YOKO ONO

The only thing you need to take to work is you

Imagine if you could work in a place where the thing everyone takes accountability for is living up to what they stand for. Not jostling for authority or getting caught up in corporate bullshit; just human beings as leaders who want to be their true, authentic selves. We often leave our authenticity at home because we perceive work, and our leadership, to be a place where our positivity gets left behind. Someone genuinely once said to me that 'you can't be positive and professional'. Seriously – what the actual fuck were they thinking?

Someone is more likely to ask you why you smile at work or be curious about why you're happy than they are to ask you why you never smile and are always miserable. People have asked me, 'Why are you so positive?' and, 'Where do you get your enthusiasm from?' Honestly? Miserable and ignorant are already taken, so I might as well be happy and engaging!

Integrity and enthusiasm is an international language.

– NOVA FERGUSON

I don't want to be miserable and ignorant! And I don't want you to be, either. I've been there, and it's shit – for me and everyone around me. It's actually much more exhausting *not* being authentic! Trying to be something you're not leads to you feeling overwhelmed and lost. Your boss and the environment you work in won't change just because you want them to – you have to change you.

No one likes a leader who is erratic, or who loses their shit when the pressure is on or when people make mistakes. The true, authentic you doesn't behave like that; the true, authentic you chooses a response that stops people turning against you as a leader and gives you the trust and rapport that you want with your team. By starting with you, you create a world where both you and your team wake up in the morning and want to go to work.

Lose your shit tomorrow.
Today is no day to fall apart.

– BUDDY DIEKER, OZARK

Leaders who break the mould see emotional humans, not staff

You are an emotional creature. There, I've said it. You, reading this book – whoever you are, wherever you are, whatever you do – you are an emotional creature. Everything you do comes from an emotional reaction that triggers your thoughts and feelings. It happens naturally, instinctively.

You are surrounded by other emotional creatures, too. Not Tim, Leila, Lynn, Matthew, Dave, Phoebe, Colin, Lucie and Margaret. Not even your mother, father, sister, brother, best friend. In work, you're not surrounded by colleagues, team members, bosses, execs, staff, employees, customers,

clients, suppliers and stakeholders; you are instead surrounded by many, many other emotional creatures. That's
what you are leading: a group of emotional creatures. Stop
seeing the people you work with as names and job titles.
They are human beings with their own hang-ups and their
own hopes and dreams.

In your next meeting or video call, look around the room
or the screen. See the other participants as the human,
emotional creatures they really are and engage with them
as your true, authentic self. The one thing you have in
common with everyone you work with is your emotions.
The success of your leadership comes from your ability to
choose a positive response to the emotional reactions that
arise in the situations you are presented with. And those
emotional reactions are triggered by what you and other
emotional creatures hear, see, feel and do. You can be as
smart, cool or as good looking as you want, but if you
can't deal with people, then you're knackered. Leadership
is about getting the basics right, and the first basic is to win
hearts and minds.

Even some of the worst experiences of leadership are determined by the emotional experience. People don't get pissed
off because you make them redundant; they get pissed off
because of how you treat them while making them redundant. Organisations spend time and money on creating ini-
tiatives to engage people. We've all seen them: free fruit,
ping-pong tables, mindfulness and yoga sessions and the

occasional give-away of free stuff. Then they moan about people leaving their organisation, and their managers end up spending more time and money on replacing the people who have left than they do on developing and leading their people.

All the free fruit in the world won't make you feel better if your manager is a prick.

People will never ever, ever, ever, ever, EVER forget the way you make them feel.

– NOEL GALLAGHER (WITH A BIG NOD TO MAYA ANGELOU)

A tale of two leaders

Let me first introduce you to my worst boss, Narcissistic Norman. As a CEO, one of Norman's traits was erratic behaviour: changing the direction of the business for no apparent reason, messaging people at 3am and expecting them to reply. Arriving at work in a brand new £120,000 car the day after over 100 of his employees had been put at risk of redundancy, completely oblivious to the message it sent to people.

When an exec or senior leader didn't do things exactly as Norman would have done them, he would call the HR manager, who would be ordered to 'Get rid of them and find me someone else.'

Norman didn't lack the ability to build a successful brand; what he lacked was the ability to recognise how his actions directly impacted on the people within his business. His lack of desire to build positive relationships cascaded through the organisation, resulting in a 60% labour turnover rate over a five-year period! His actions were a direct result of his inability to choose a positive response to his thoughts and feelings, his inability to start with himself. Running a business is hard; being a decent human being is much easier.

Contrast Narcissistic Norman with Josh, who made positive choices for himself and his team to break the mould. Josh was newly promoted to a senior leadership role. I worked with him on an Enthuse leadership programme and, at the end of our six months working together, Josh shared how he had transformed his days and his relationships with his team.

Josh would previously spend a lot of time chasing people up and micromanaging his team because he expected them to work in the exact same way as him. If people didn't reply to emails or pick up customer requests as quickly as he would have done, then he would either end up doing it for them or would awkwardly approach the situation, creating difficult conversations.

Through learning about how to focus on himself and how he could apply it in his role, he was able to recognise that he was causing problems for himself by imposing his own way of working on others. Josh took a step back and recognised that the reality was that his team were performing, and it was his own feelings of uncertainty and insecurity as a leader that were leading to him feeling negative emotions and prompting difficult conversations.

Josh changed his approach by recognising his emotions, understanding the thoughts and feelings that came with them, and choosing a positive response. When he better understood his negative emotions and how to respond to them, he could instead spend his time reviewing how he and his team could improve their service. This ensured they could have more of an impact on the business, doing the important work they wanted to do instead of getting lost in the minutiae of every task– tasks that would get done regardless of whether Josh stressed out over them or not.

The conversations with his team were now positive and focused on what support they needed from him, and he was able to give effective feedback without upsetting anyone. That led to positive change, with his team taking responsibility for the solutions. Josh and his team were now happy and enjoying open and honest conversations.

Josh's transformation is made more remarkable when we consider that he started the leadership programme by saying he wanted to get better at time management. He later commented that 'managing your time means nothing if you can't manage your emotions.'

That's leadership, right there: a leader who can positively influence their own emotional reactions *and* those of others. Someone who can give critical feedback and still build relationships. That is where we want to work, that is how we break the mould – no blame cultures, no petty squabbles, no favouritism, no dishonesty, just a culture where we can be ourselves because we recognise the importance of positively influencing our instinctive emotional reactions.

**You are not your thoughts;
you are your choices.**

Breaking the mould keeps you happy in your job: Incompetent Ian

Let me reintroduce you to Incompetent Ian. Ian was a director of recruitment and training, and his inability to choose a positive response to his world meant he had been moved from pillar to post across many roles in the organisation, often being moved to another role to hide his incompetence. It was only his personal relationship with the owner of the business that had saved him from losing his job. He was someone who perfectly fitted the mould that others made for him.

The period I spent working with Ian was littered with frustration and my own time being wasted; he often set us off on projects that never went anywhere because he quickly moved his attention to something else. I remember spending two months creating a plan for how we could commercialise our training offering. When I presented it to Ian, he simply said, 'Oh, we're not doing that any more.'

Ian managed to completely alienate his entire leadership team when he insisted that we all clear our diaries for a 'weekly management meeting' that was absolutely sacrosanct. The title of the meeting says it all; if we were allowed to get on with our jobs, we wouldn't need a weekly meeting to discuss what we needed to manage! The first meeting came around and, after working long hours to prepare for it, the rest of the leadership team and I arrived only to be told by his PA (who was also his wife!) that Ian wouldn't be attending because 'something more important' had come up that he had to deal with.

Ian wasn't known as incompetent because he lacked the experience or knowledge to lead a recruitment and training team, or because he hadn't had any leadership training. It was because of his complete lack of awareness and his inability to choose a positive response to the situations that his incompetence put him in. He completely lacked the desire and ability to motivate himself to lead people and didn't have a sliver of empathy within him, so couldn't see how annoying his actions were for others. Ian thought the right thing to do was to fit the mould, because that's what his thoughts and feelings told him to do. My final interaction with Ian came with this exchange on my last day with the organisation:

Ian: 'So, how long have you been here, Tim?'

Me: 'Six years.'

Ian (letting out a big sigh): 'Six years, eh? I've done 26 years, and I don't know if it's all been worth it.'

Imagine dedicating 26 years of your life to working for an organisation and you don't know if it was worth it? Fuck that!

**And you've got to lead where
your heart says go
And in hope that it turns out so
And that's all you can hope for
Can you expect much more?**

— THE STYLE COUNCIL

You always have a choice

**People rebel against your behaviour,
not against you.**

If anyone reading this book wants to be more like Narcissistic Norman or Incompetent Ian, then you're reading the wrong book! Being able to respond positively to your thoughts and feelings gives you freedom from negative thoughts and self-doubt. It shows you there is another way to behave and operate as a leader. Your emotions and the accompanying thoughts and feelings can hold you back.

It's those thoughts and feelings that tell you to go to every meeting and send lots of emails, to micromanage your team and take out your frustrations on other people. When you start with you, then you are able to experience those thoughts and feelings and choose how to respond to them.

Choosing to start with you sends you forward and empowers you to stop worrying about what everyone else is doing and what they think of you, and to get on with doing what you want to do as a leader instead. It shows you that you are in complete control of choosing to be your best version of you. It always starts with you.

Smile again

Smile again

One day I hope

To make you smile again.

– MICHAEL KIWANUKA

I have included, at the end of the book, my top 10 books (and records!) to help you to break the mould, including my tribute to those who have inspired me to be my best version of me.

To make sure it always starts with you, use your *Break the Mould* workbook. If you haven't got it yet, you can buy one from **www.italwaysstartswithyou.com** and make your own positive choices.

So what?

➡ You have to make your leadership always start with you.

➡ You and the people you lead are not their names or job titles; they are emotional creatures.

➡ You can be as smart, cool or as good looking as you want; if you can't deal with people, you're knackered.

➡ It's not about what you know; it's about the choices you make.

➡ Trying to be something you're not leads to you feeling overwhelmed and lost.

➡ You always have a choice.

Get enthused

➡ What choices are you making to be happy as a leader?

➡ What are the positive attitudes or behaviours that you want to demonstrate as a leader?

➡ How well do you already recognise and understand your emotions?

➡ What are you going to do to break the moulds that are set for you?

➡ How self-aware are you?

➡ How are you going to show up at work as your true, authentic self?

CHAPTER 4

MY STORY: HOW I BECAME MY BEST VERSION OF ME

I was not born
Into this world
To do another man's bidding.

– FONTAINES DC

Well, who are you?

I want to share my story with you. Don't worry– this isn't like the other books you've read where you take a detour while the author tells you all about the success they've had and how you should follow the same path. I'll keep it focused on how I changed as a leader rather than telling you how wonderful I am. The book isn't about me; it's about you. I want to share my story with you because I've been there – bad bosses, making mistakes, feeling stressed, moving jobs and having difficult conversations, wondering why I ever became a leader.

The most important story you will ever read is your own.

I haven't always been a coach and inspirational speaker. I was another young manager who had my hopes and aspirations kicked out of me and lost my enthusiasm as I experienced the realities of leadership. My leadership career started in the same way as it does for many others when I was asked to manage the team I was part of. This promotion was based purely on my work ethic as a 'doer'. When I look back at me then, a naïve 21-year-old, no way was I ready to become a leader of people; being a 'doer' and working long hours are not the qualities of a good leader!

But that initial promotion prompted a promising leadership career. I progressed everywhere I worked, and followed the archetypal path as I moved up the levels of leadership, climbing the corporate ladder. Many times, I celebrated a promotion and pay rise and got excited about my future, expecting big things ahead. Periods of success were plentiful, yet they were always followed by periods of desperation and wondering what the hell I was doing and how I ended up where I was. It would be fair to say that my early leadership career was a mixed bag of hard work, optimism, disenchantment and, to be really blunt, some proper dog-shit times. I can vividly remember a recurring thought: *surely, work isn't supposed to be like this*. Hindsight really is a wonderful thing, and I can see clearly now that I was my own villain; I was failing to develop my self-awareness and blaming others for my experiences, which was the cause of my roller coaster of emotions and experiences.

My story can be summed up by telling you that I went from being my own villain to my own hero. To give you a very brief history of my story as a leader, it can be split into two parts: fitting the mould and breaking the mould. Here's a summary (in no particular order) of my experiences in those parts of my story:

FITTING THE MOULD	BREAKING THE MOULD
Working long hours	Productive days
Stress, anxiety and depression	Enjoying my family time
Sleepless nights	Turning my work phone off when I got home

FITTING THE MOULD	BREAKING THE MOULD
Upsetting my wife and kids because I was going home angry and fed up with work	Spending my time and energy on the things that add value to me and my team
Having my trust and work ethic taken advantage of	Focussing on the things within my control
Seeing my boss take credit for my work	Saying 'no' to the crap that others threw at me
Losing weekends to negative thoughts and feelings of how much I dreaded Monday mornings	Being able to ignore the incompetence of others and concentrate on my own behaviours and performance
Feeling like I always had to be available	Declining meeting invites for boring or pointless meetings
Experiencing the same frustrations with other people over and over again	Making my meetings engaging and effective
Having my time and energy wasted time and time again by the incompetence of others	Becoming clear on my values, purpose and refusing to compromise them
Feeling like it was only me that cared and that I was the only one that had problems as a leader	Finding my real passion and going after my ambitions

FITTING THE MOULD	BREAKING THE MOULD
Lack of personal purpose and imposter syndrome leaving me feeling like a failure and that 'I might get found out as a leader'	Taking positive risks to carve out the career that I wanted
Being told 'you could stop acting like such a shithouse all the time' by a member of my team	In control of where my time and energy spent
	Asking for feedback and acting on it
	Refusing to get caught up in the bullshit of office politics

Just from reading those experiences, you can tell that the version of me in the first column needed to change. I was sleepwalking into a career of unhappiness, and choosing to break the mould woke me up.

When routine bites hard and ambitions are low And resentment rides high,

**but emotions won't grow
And we're changing our ways,
taking different roads.**

– JOY DIVISION

Ch-ch-ch-ch-changes

**There's gonna have to be a different man
Time may change me
But I can't trace time.**

– DAVID BOWIE

It's important to state at this point that, when anyone is feeling like there is more to life and that they're destined for more, they need a catalyst— something to create that spark within them, the self-motivation to not only know that enough is enough and that things need to change, but to actually do something about it. It's that something that slaps us in the face and shows us that we are in control of making the change we need to make and deciding what happens next.

"I didn't need my boss's or anyone else's permission. I needed my own permission to break the mould and change myself for the better."

You can wait for a lifetime, to spend your days in the sunshine. When it comes on top, you've gotta make it happen.

– OASIS

My catalyst for change came in the shape of a book and the most inspirational leader I have ever worked with. They showed me how to stop being my own villain and put my time and energy into becoming my best version of me.

Like a lot of leaders, I'd attended training sessions where we were told about effective tools we could use. One that stood out to me was Stephen Covey and his *Seven Habits of Highly Effective People*. I remember leaving a training course after being introduced to Covey's approach and being excited to learn more; I ordered the book that night. When it arrived in the post, I looked at the cover and read the introduction, thinking it would be the book that would help me to be a better leader. And then I put it on a shelf and never did anything else with it.

I finally picked it up again (literally blowing the dust off the cover!) when my optimism was back and I had the motivation to change– and change me it certainly did. Cliché alert: reading that book changed my life. It made me realise why people behave the way they do and how I was spending far too much time trying to please people who didn't really care about me and choosing to neglect the thing that would have the biggest impact on my leadership – me. The book taught me so much about myself and, as I started to learn more about myself, it made me wonder why I was leaving my personal values and beliefs at home and, instead, trying to fit the mould and live up to what I perceived as the expectations of me as a manager.

That nagging thought that things should be different made me realise I was always waiting for permission: permission to have a meeting with my boss, permission to lead my team the way I wanted to lead them… I was even waiting for other people to give me permission to be myself. When you start to pay attention to those nagging thoughts, you start to notice the things that don't sit right with you, and it stirs your motivation to think differently and to seek opportunities to make things better for you and those that you lead.

I didn't need my boss's or anyone else's permission. I needed my own permission to break the mould and change myself for the better.

I am not a product of my circumstances. I am a product of my decisions.

– STEPHEN COVEY

And then along came Zoe Sinclair. In our careers, we all need *the one* – that one leader we work with who shows us that things can be different. Someone who challenges us and makes us think differently. Zoe was the one who did that for me. If you haven't found that one yet, then keep looking, because they are out there. Zoe made me want to break the mould.

Zoe was head of organisational development where I worked. She had invited me to attend a leadership workshop that she was running, as she thought I would benefit from joining. I was sceptical and told her that the previous training I'd had didn't really do anything for me. Zoe's response has now become a positive mantra that I say to myself when I doubt whether or not I should do something for the first time: 'There's only one way to find out.'

Zoe's approach to the workshop had an impact on me like no one had ever had. She told us that 'as a leader, you have to start with you'. The first words she said to us were,

'These two days are not about leadership theories, they're about you.' Instead of showing us some PowerPoint slides and telling us what we would learn, she wrote two questions on a flipchart and told us to get in pairs to discuss our answers:

➡ What's important to you?

➡ What would you want the people you lead to say about you to your family and friends?

I was hooked! I worked with Zoe for two days, and she changed my view of leadership and the way I viewed myself. She made me think about how the choices I was making were leading to my negative experiences, and she intro-duced me to the fact that I could choose a positive response to my thoughts and feelings. I learnt that I was blaming others and my circumstances for how I was feeling, and I understood how unhelpful that was. I learnt that I could break the mould, that I could make choices to respond pos-itively to my thoughts and feelings. Zoe showed me that I could stop trying to be like everyone else.

**No one ever changed the
world by being normal.**

– PETER HOOK

Spending that time with Zoe showed me that it always starts with you (I actually wrote those words for the first time during those two days with Zoe). It made me realise that I can choose to work hard and be inspired to lead myself and those around me *despite* what my boss says or what the environment or culture is doing. This was so refreshing; all the other leadership development training I'd experienced had told me to make others work hard and that I needed to motivate *them* to do their own jobs. But Zoe's approach flipped it for me: I realised that I needed to work hard for myself, because the only person I could really motivate was me.

The concept of being able to choose how I responded to my thoughts and feelings was like finding the keys to utopia, because it showed me that I could think differently and that it was up to me to define what happened. I stopped worrying about what other people were doing or thinking about me, and focused on me; I became appropriately selfish to develop my best version of me. For me, this was the missing link in becoming an inspirational leader and a more contented human.

With the realisation that I was in control of how I responded to my thoughts and feelings, my self-talk changed. The most important person you'll ever have a conversation with is the one who looks back at you from the mirror. I realised that I had been telling myself the wrong things, both about myself and my team, because of the emotions that were triggered when I was trying to fit the mould, aligning myself with the environment and culture where I worked – not with my best version of me.

I stopped doing exactly what my boss told me to do. All they really cared about was that I did a good job to make them look good; they didn't actually care how I did it. I made sure it was my own voice that was in my head, not theirs. I started to recognise that there was a direct correlation between the number of years you had spent in a business and how cynical you became. I was on that path to cynicism, and I had to make changes. I had to start to focus on living up to what I stood for and being responsible for what happened as a result of doing that. I realised that I didn't need to study leadership; I needed to get off my arse and do it! Then I could get on with being me.

By choosing positive responses to my thoughts and feelings, I could now see that my behaviour as a manager came from fear – the fear of letting go, the fear of judgement by others, the fear of trusting others to make decisions and the fear of not living up to the perceived expectations of me as a manager.

**Don't just be another guy chasing
a stupid number.**

– THE ROLLING STONES

Make wise decisions based on your own experiences, not just what other people tell you

Just because I started to choose positive responses to my thoughts and feelings doesn't mean everyone else changed and the world became sunshine and cocktails every day. Not at all – I was the only one on my own journey of change, and it showed me that you have to get up every day prepared to work hard and to keep having conversations, continuing to break the mould.

Remember that there is no such thing as a quick win in leadership and there is no guaranteed way to lead people – because people are people and all of us are different and need different things from our leaders. Leadership takes hard work, commitment and time.

I shifted my attitudes and behaviours to being my best version of me and made different choices:

➡ I chose to get absolute clarity on what I stood for.

➡ I chose to get to know my team and what they needed from me.

➡ I chose to collaboratively create the environment that people wanted to work in.

➡ I chose to listen to people.

➡ I chose to empathise with people.

➡ I chose to be self-motivated.

➡ I chose not to react to my negative emotional triggers.

➡ I chose not to allow the behaviours of others and the environment to determine how I behaved.

➡ I chose to engage with myself and to always take my personal values and beliefs into work.

➡ I chose to inspire myself and take a positive outlook.

➡ I chose to build relationships that made me smile, not scowl.

I started to be able to recognise my emotional reactions and listen to my thoughts and feelings and decide what would happen next. That's what breaking the mould does;

no matter what is happening, it enables you to stop and understand how you're feeling and what you want to happen next. It always puts you in control.

**And everyone seems just like me,
They struggle hard to set themselves free,
And they're waiting for the change.**

– THE JAM

It's not about doing something; it's about letting go

As I made the positive choices that come from breaking the mould, I let go of control. Letting go meant that the results we were getting as a team went from being OK to exceeding expectations. I changed my awareness back to me. I used to walk into work expecting people to make mistakes, waiting and watching for them to do something wrong, or not in the exact same way or at the same speed as I would do it. I turned that back to me and asked, 'What do I need from the team?' More importantly, I asked myself, 'What do they need from me?' Then I focused my awareness on how I needed to come across to achieve what we wanted to achieve.

I used to stress over the minutiae of everything my team did. Now, I was having conversations with them about what they wanted from their roles, and they were putting in discretionary effort and thinking for themselves. Whereas I used to spend Friday afternoons producing perfunctory reports that analysed our results, and would email them out to everyone with some passive-aggressive comments that I thought were motivational, now my team were the ones producing the results of their hard work and excitedly telling me what we had achieved every week.

We went from meeting expectations and constantly working in 'urgent mode' to never missing a KPI and being invited to help other teams improve their performance. In fact, we were now being included in new contracts being set up because, in the words of one senior leader, 'Tim's team won't let us down, and we need them involved as early as possible when we bring on new customers.'

I took my personal development seriously. I started to journal my experiences and reflect on my impact on others. I started practising mindfulness and became a voracious reader, learning more and more about how to choose a positive response to my thoughts and feelings. I asked my boss and my team for feedback and acted on it, despite how much the thought of their feedback scared me! I got myself mentors for the first time and spent time learning more about me and my personal purpose.

I realised that the environment and other people weren't going to change, so I had to change. The change in me was to choose positive emotions and be aware of how I wanted to respond to my thoughts and feelings. It got my boss off my back. The change in me galvanised the aspirational members of my team, who now had a leader to look up to. It gained me respect from the 'I just do my job and go home' members of the team and enabled me to engage more with the youngest members, who previously just saw me as 'the boss' and someone to be avoided.

It's quite amazing the response you get when you choose to just be you. Not only were my team happier and more successful, but I was no longer stressed and going home bloody miserable. I stopped micromanaging my team and trusted them to get on with it. The whole dynamic of our communication changed. We were no longer under the microscope from my boss, because our performance exceeded expectations. Our reputation blossomed, which sent the message that we built positive relationships and would stand up to any challenges we faced, including office politics or being blamed for things not going well. It felt like I'd gone from working in a vicious circle to being in an environment of empowerment.

Other managers in the business started to ask me for advice and would proactively work with my team instead of working in silos. We adopted an approach of 'put down the mouse and pick up the phone'; instead of being keyboard warriors, we built relationships with people inside and outside of the business, so we became the team that people came to for help and to understand how we did things. They even asked why we all seemed so happy!

Of course, there was some backlash as a result of the success my team and I were now having. Some managers clearly felt threatened by me and would look for every chance to prove that we had done something wrong. I could handle that now, though, and preferred it to some of the clashes I used to experience. In fact, the backlash was actually a blessing, because it meant I got invited to fewer meetings that were a waste of my time; instead of sitting in meetings listening to people flex their authority and argue over who was doing what, I could now focus my time on me and my team.

I stopped giving a shit about being in every meeting for the fear of missing out, and found that being my authentic self led to me being able to recognise that people will react the way they choose to react; all I can do is be myself and live up to what I stand for. When I started doing that, people left me to get on with it, because they saw that it worked and appreciated the positive influence I was having on myself and those around me.

**Life will bring you pain by itself;
your job is to find joy.**

– MILTON ERICKSON

*It doesn't matter what your job title is. First
and foremost, you're a human being. You
can control your own behaviour.*

You may be reading this and thinking, 'You achieved all
that just by breaking the mould?' Yes, I did – because when
you are able to make positive choices to respond to your
thoughts and feelings, you improve your interpersonal skills
and manage your negative emotions to be more effective.
You can have all the skills and knowledge in the world, but
if you can't choose how to respond to the thoughts and
feelings that you experience from your emotions, those
skills and your knowledge are redundant. In the real world,
you will encounter unexpected challenges, difficult people,
opposition to your ideas, toxic cultures and periods of self-
doubt. Breaking the mould means that you never let them
take you off course from being your true, authentic self.

Sometimes I wish I could go back in time and give myself
advice before becoming a leader, or go back and tell the

younger me how to behave. However, I'm actually glad I can't, because I'd rather have had the experiences and learnt from them than not have them. All I can do now is be my best version of me, and people will know the true me.

Breaking the mould doesn't make you the world's greatest leader or coach, and it definitely doesn't make you better than anyone else. It enables you to make positive choices to be your best version of you. That's all anyone else can ever ask of you. It always starts with you.

There is no going backwards – only forward.

– PAUL WELLER

The challenge is the opportunity

Now I am a coach and inspirational speaker. All of the shit times I had as a leader and the changes I made brought me to where I am today. Zoe wasn't just the amazing trainer at a leadership course; she was the one who encouraged me to take the risk of going into learning and development for the first time and to give up the empire I was building thanks to the changes I made by breaking the mould.

From taking that risk, I discovered my passion for helping other people to break the mould and sharing how you can choose to be your best version of you. Not a keyboard warrior or a member of the uniform police, checking the colour of people's shoes. And definitely not the version of you who fits the mould and is lost as a leader, yearning for something else.

I never looked back. I threw myself into every challenge I faced in my new role and had more determination to help others than I'd ever had before. That's what I found was my real driving force – not the chance to do the 'pink and fluffy' work in a people-focused role, and I wasn't even doing it just to work with Zoe and get away from the dickheads and the corporate bullshit. I genuinely had a purpose to help as many leaders as possible.

From my experience of going from stressed-out, overwhelmed manager to being my best version of me as a leader, I kept thinking, 'I can't be the only one,' and sought out as many opportunities as possible to support leaders in learning more about themselves and becoming more authentic. I could see that a lot of managers were miserable because they were trying to fit themselves into a mould that would never suit them, and I wanted to help as many of them as possible to break the mould.

I worked harder than I'd ever worked before, giving up my weekends to study and become qualified in coaching, learning design and emotional intelligence. I had the bug and didn't want to let anything stop me. This was all part of me breaking the mould, because I'd never committed to my personal development before; I pushed myself harder than I'd ever done before and took every opportunity to get out of my comfort zone. I realised that you could do a good job while learning and developing yourself. I was better able to deal with the stress and pressure of a busy job, being a parent, having a life and learning, because breaking the mould enabled me to make positive choices.

My motivation was higher than ever before, because I realised that my best version of me would be enough. It's all anyone really needs. Being that best version of me was how I could do a better job than ever before while challenging and developing myself. I was no longer chasing a promotion or the next pay rise; I wanted to learn more about myself and help others. That's the feeling I want to give you – to help you enjoy your work and be your best version of you.

Nothing can dim the light that shines from within.

– MAYA ANGELOU

Gaining more and more experience in working with other leaders led me to change my thinking and embrace my biggest challenges as my biggest opportunities. I'd spent many years avoiding challenges as a leader and learning nothing about myself as a result. Now I had the desire to be true to myself and face those challenges head on, helping others to make positive choices in the process.

Sometimes, as a coach and facilitator, you only get one chance to make a positive impression, and I started to take those chances in whatever situation I faced. Let me tell you about some of my favourite challenges.

Barry from Carlisle

Barry from Carlisle— that's how he introduced himself to me!— turned up for a leadership workshop, and straight away he made it clear that he was going to be difficult. As I went to collect the group from the waiting area and invite them to join me in the training room, Barry physically blocked my way, squaring up to me, and said, 'I don't even know why I'm here.' He was clearly trying to stare me down.

Barry remained difficult through the morning and pissed other people off. Despite his negative attitude, all I could do was role model positive behaviour. There was no point confronting him or letting him ruin it for everyone else. I wanted to be the best version of myself to invite Barry to be the best version of himself, and made sure he was included. But he sat on his chair, arms crossed, shoulders slumped, being difficult. I was determined to get him on board and get those shoulders up.

And it worked. At the right time, I asked him an open question, and he discovered the real problem for himself: Barry didn't like his boss and was taking it out on his team. He opened up and took responsibility to change things for himself and his team. At the end of the day, he thanked me and apologised for his behaviour earlier in the day. Another attendee said to me, 'I can't believe how well you handled him.'

Death-stare Kev

Have you ever worked with a group of people when one member of the group is reluctant to contribute and spends the day staring at you like they want to kill you? Death-stare Kev gave me such an experience during a coaching workshop.

While this was quite strange behaviour to demonstrate at a coaching workshop and was quite disconcerting for me, I made sure not to judge Kev and focused on creating a positive environment for everyone to learn more about how to coach their teams.

When the day ended, Kev approached me, thanked me and told me how much he'd enjoyed the day and how much he'd got from it. I thanked him and told him that I appreciated his feedback; I also asked if I could give him some feedback. It went along the lines of, 'Thanks for that feedback, Kev – maybe next time tell your face that you're enjoying it!' I shared with him how his face had suggested that he'd had a completely different experience and told him that he'd appeared to be giving me a death stare all day.

To his credit, Kev accepted my feedback, assuring me that it was his 'thinking face' and that I should not take it personally. I told him it was OK with me and that I wanted to take the opportunity to make him aware of it in case he was doing that in meetings with his team.

A few weeks later, Kev sent me an email thanking me for my feedback and shared how he'd asked his team for feedback on how he appears in meetings. They had given him similar feedback and told him how his apparent attitude sometimes held them back from sharing their ideas with him. Kev was now working on being more aware of his non-verbal communication; my feedback had enabled him to have more open conversations with his team, so they weren't judging his response just from the look on his face.

Even if you do look at someone like you want to kill them, if no one tells you then you can't do anything about it!

Big Mick

'You've got Big Mick with you tomorrow, Tim – good luck.' That was the message I got from a colleague as I prepared to deliver a presentation skills course. Big Mick had a reputation, and my colleague was trying to get me to assume that his reputation meant bad news for me. My response was, 'Right, cool. I've never met him before, so I'll see how we get on.'

Big Mick did his best to live up to his reputation by telling me during the first activity on the day, 'I've heard all this before, mate. I work with hairy-arsed working-class lads. You can't teach me anything new.' To me, this came across like he was trying to assert his authority in the room rather than actually having any issue with me, and I replied, 'Thanks for sharing that, Mick. Just to be clear– I'm not here to "teach" you anything. My job is to share the content and facilitate the activities. You decide what you do with it afterwards. If that's how you feel about today, what are you doing here, mate?'

Mick clearly liked that I had risen to his challenge, and he thought about it for a few seconds before letting out a little nervous laugh and admitting, 'I keep getting told that my daily briefings are crap, so I asked my boss for help and he sent me on this course.'

Mick being able to share that with the group changed the atmosphere, and everyone relaxed. My view was that I was not going to judge Mick based on what others told me about him or because of his behaviour. After all, learning experiences are out of many people's comfort zones, and people behave uncharacteristically in reaction to negative emotional triggers.

The course ended and Mick was the star of the show, putting lots of hard work into making his daily briefings more engaging, and I later got really positive feedback from his boss about how Mick had changed as a result of the workshop. Mick left the course by giving me a really firm handshake and telling me in his own inimitable style, 'You're fucking wasted here, lad.'

People are good, basically.
They just need to be shown.

— BILLY CONNOLLY

I'm not sharing those stories because I'm the best coach or facilitator or because I can do things better than others. I'm sharing them because I broke the mould and chose a positive response to my thoughts and feelings. My responses, and the positive outcome in each situation, are due to breaking the mould because, believe me, what was expected of me would have meant taking a very different approach. When I fed back what had happened to my boss and colleagues at the time, these are the reactions I got:

➡ Barry from Carlisle – I was told that I should have kicked him off the course and phoned HR.

➡ Death-stare Kev – I got asked why I had given him that feedback. They advised me that speaking openly like that could get me into trouble if the feedback got taken the wrong way.

➡ Big Mick – I got a roll of the eyes from the colleague who had previously warned me about Mick. Then I got taken to one side by my boss, who asked me not to deal with situations like that, and I quote, 'because it makes the rest of the team look bad'!

Imagine if I had fitted those moulds! I would have had a very awkward conversation with HR about Barry, which would have benefited no one and seen nothing good come of it. Kev would have gone back to work still giving his team the death stare and struggling to build rapport. Big Mick would have turned up at the next training course giving other people grief to mask his own insecurity and still not changing his behaviour.

It was those experiences that made me realise that taking a teaching or telling approach to leadership development, or the classic 'death by PowerPoint' approach, just doesn't work. It will only ever take people so far. You need to create a learning experience that makes them think differently. One that makes Barry from Carlisle hold the mirror up to himself; that enables Big Mick to drop the bravado; that helps Death-stare Kev consider how he comes across to others. That's only achieved when you create the environment for leaders to go beyond their perceptions and break the mould by making positive choices.

Those three examples highlight the need to break the mould and be who you truly are. No one benefits from all of us always fitting into the mould that others create for us. By breaking the mould in those situations, I was able to recognise that Barry, Kev and Big Mick were simply reacting to their thoughts and feelings. I chose to make a positive response to my own emotions, which turned those potentially disastrous experiences into ones where people learnt about themselves and built better relationships as a result.

**Never knew what a world this was
'Til I looked in my heart
Saw myself for what I am
Found a whole world in my hand.**

– PAUL WELLER

Doing what I'm supposed to be doing

Just find what makes you happy
and do it 'til you're gone.

– JASON ISBELL

That experience of going from being a fed-up leader to breaking the mould can be the trigger for finding your passion. Once you get a passion for something, you can't look back. You can't half-arse it. You have to go for it.

I left full-time employment and created Enthuse to help people break the mould and be their best version of themselves. Instead of being faced with narcissistic nobheads and corporate bullshit, now I work with individuals and leadership teams, coaching them to break the mould, and with organisations who genuinely want their staff to feel positive and have the balls to try a new way of doing things. My days are spent providing four key solutions:

➡ Enthuse Coaching

➡ Enthuse Inspirational Talks

➡ Enthuse Your Leadership

➡ Enthuse Tours

My coaching clients go on a journey of self-discovery with me and break the mould by reconnecting with who they are, being more authentic so they can be the leader they want to be. My inspirational talks light up company events and big conferences, inspiring people to make positive choices. My Enthuse Your Leadership programmes take a group coaching approach, underpinned by emotional intelligence. The Enthuse Tours give people and teams a space to be themselves, engage in group coaching and learn from their peers. These experiences turn managers into inspirational, self-aware leaders who give a shit about their teams and have the conversations that matter.

Ultimately, when you get enthused by breaking the mould, you get to be more authentic and be your best version of you. This makes you happier and more fulfilled and turns your team and organisation into a place where people want to work.

I want to help as many people as possible— and I don't think that's too lofty a goal, is it? Why can't I work with coaching clients who want to be their true, authentic selves? Why can't I work with organisations that want their leaders to be happy? I want to work with organisations and leaders who want positive cultures and who want their people to be their best version of themselves. Instead of suffering in toxic cultures, I now help leaders and organisations to create environments that are values-led and to create engagement. These are places where people can choose to be their authentic selves.

Don't just take my word for it. Check out the testimonials on my website from my coaching clients and the leaders I have worked with, or my LinkedIn recommendations. I can tell you whatever you want about what I do and how I do it, but it's more important for me to let my work do the talking for me. In Part Two, I have included inspirational real-life stories from some of my coaching clients who share their experiences of working with me, and there are examples of real leaders who have broken the mould by getting enthused.

My desire to help leaders and organisations comes from my own experience; I know that it's so easy to fall into dick-head behaviour. All the dickheads will be just fine whatever you choose to do. You have to make the choices that are right for you. When you do that, you are the leader that you and your team want you to be.

You've got two choices in life – have a go or don't have a go. You'll always learn more by having a go.

I find it so rewarding to help people break the mould by:

➡ Choosing a positive response to their thoughts and feelings

➡ Stopping overthinking things and focusing, instead, on what's important

➡ Gaining the confidence to be the leader they want to be

➡ Having the leadership conversations that matter

➡ Leading a high-performing team

➡ Overcoming their limiting beliefs

➡ Self-coaching to make positive choices

➡ Developing and applying emotional intelligence

➡ Becoming more self-aware

➡ Being their true authentic selves

➡ Being enthused and building positive relationships

What gives me the most satisfaction with Enthuse is helping others to have a similar positive experience to me. Breaking the mould made me realise that I have a choice, that I'm in control of what happens to me and the work that I do. Yes,

I worked hard. Yes, I built networks. Yes, I got qualified. Yes, I challenged myself and gained experience. Without breaking the mould, I wouldn't have done any of that.

The moral of my story is that without breaking the mould I would be in a job I hated, working for an organisation that I didn't respect, with a boss who didn't care, surrounded by miserable people... NO THANKS!

Top tips to break the mould for your own story

TOP TIP	HOW IT HELPS TO BREAK THE MOULD
Take your personal development seriously	Ensures that you continue to evolve and don't allow others to tell you how to develop
Get clear on your personal purpose	Makes sure that the time and energy you commit to your work aligns with what you want from your life
Find your passion	Keeps you motivated to do what you're supposed to be doing and steers you away from getting stuck in a mould set for you by others

Focus on making positive choices	Helps you to choose to do what is right for you as a leader, not what everyone else tells you to do
Remember that you are only responsible for your own behaviour	Stops you stressing over what others are doing and makes you focus on your own behaviour
Make sure it's your own voice in your head	Builds your confidence to be yourself and stops you allowing others to tell you who you are

Please stop tryin' to impress the people who don't care about you, I repeat as a mantra.

– SAM FENDER

I want this book to help you break the mould and choose the moral of your own story. Use it to coach yourself to be the best version of you that you want to be. You don't need to swallow a self-help manual or be able to recite leadership theory; you need to make positive choices.

Get in touch with me at tim.roberts@enthusecoaching.com to see how I can help you and your organisation to break the mould.

Success is doing what you love and being happy doing it.

– JOHNNY MARR

So what?

➡ Getting promoted because you're good at your core job does not make you a good leader.

➡ Leadership takes hard work, commitment and time.

➡ Fitting the mould leads to bad days and breaking the mould leads to good days.

➡ You don't need anyone's permission to break the mould.

➡ You have to lead based on what is important to you.

➡ The challenge is the opportunity.

Get enthused

➡ What's important to you?

➡ What would you want the people you lead to say about you to your family and friends?

➡ What is it that you're supposed to be doing?

➡ What do you want to make happen for you?

➡ What are you doing to create a positive environment for you and those you lead?

➡ What positive choices are you already making as a leader?

PART TWO

HOW TO BREAK THE
MOULD AND BE THE BEST
VERSION OF YOU

INTRODUCTION
TO PART TWO

Congratulations— now you've reached the liberation part! Part One set the context and showed us the dangers of fitting the mould; Part Two shows you how to break the mould. We're going to take your awareness and motivation from Part One and turn it into something that makes a difference for you and those around you.

Part Two is the learning bit – the practical stuff to enable you to make a change in the real world. I am going to introduce you to some ideas that will ignite your self-awareness superpower and enable you to truly inspire others. I want you to be able to self-coach as a result of reading this book and using the workbook. In fact, I have chosen the ideas that I will be sharing with you specifically because I believe you can do them for yourself and you can use them with your teams. I'll also share some inspirational examples of leaders who have broken the mould, highlighting the value of being your true, authentic self.

**If you could be anyone
Would you choose to be yourself?
If you could be anything?
Would you still be human?**

– AFFLECK'S PALACE

Are you ready to take another path?

This part of the book is all about getting you out of the mould. When I first started writing these chapters, I found myself trying to create some sort of supermodel for you. To fit my ideas into a 'style' or 'theory' for you to digest and then go and put into practice. To be honest, my first attempt at it was a bit shit and sounded nothing like me. In fact, I was trying so hard not to be another 'leadership guru' that I was turning into exactly what I didn't want to be – I was trying to fit the mould! Then I got over myself (with a kick up the arse from my mentor and writing coach – hello, Aimee and Leila) and I remembered that the whole point of the book was to break the mould and start with you. The last thing you need is another bloody leadership model to try and follow!

I am going to share some really effective, simple ideas you can use to break the mould. This is not another leadership book that gathers dust on your shelf while you go back to doing what you've always done. The ideas are practical and applicable, unlike the grandiose theories that mean bugger all when you're faced with the same old shit on a Monday morning.

My approach is to put you at the centre of it and use original, no-bullshit content to help you change your thinking and choose how you want to come across as a leader. All the ideas I will share with you are real examples of how I work with coaching clients and leadership teams. They're not intended for you to suddenly become drastically different or perfect; they're intended to help you make the choices that you need to make to become your best version of you. Use them to guide your thinking. Use them to choose a positive response. Use them to raise your awareness. Use them to have a positive influence. Use them to build value-adding relationships. Use them to break the mould.

We'll take a simple, straightforward approach, and I will share ideas with you that will keep the process focused on you. I will tell it how it is, leaving the buzzword bingo for those who don't have the courage to break the mould.

This isn't a teaching book. It's a coaching book that makes you think about leadership and how it always starts with you. You have no right to tell others what to say or do if you haven't sorted yourself out first. Only when you have helped yourself to be happy and productive can you hope to achieve that with others. I aim to keep things really simple and show you how to break the mould by splitting it into two parts:

1. **You** – it always starts with you, and you must sort out your own shit first before you help others.

2. **Others** – we will inspire others by getting you out of the mindset that it is other people who need to change first.

Let's take a quick look at what is involved in the two parts and what they will do for you to break the mould.

You

You have to work on you first. Without this, the whole thing doesn't work. Go right back to Chapter 1 and the problem with leadership training and books; they don't start with you, and breaking the mould always starts with you. It grows your self-awareness. Without this, you won't be authentic, people will see straight through you, and you won't be happy.

This first part gets you engaged with you. Sometimes when I talk to people about this for the first time, they look at me as if they're thinking, 'get engaged with me? What is this guy smoking?' That vexed reaction comes from fitting the mould of thinking leadership, coaching and training is supposed to be about getting others to do what you want them to do. They expect me to tell them exactly how to tell others what to do and how to behave. We're not going there. We're going where it always needs to start: with you.

To start with you, I'll introduce you to two ideas that enhance your self-awareness and empower you to make positive choices. You will create your Map of the World to get clarity on what you stand for, what your purpose is and what your emotive drivers are. This shows you why your thoughts and feelings are what they are and informs how you choose to respond to them. Then you'll start to Ask Yourself First, to master your self-talk and inspire yourself by putting you in control of what happens to you.

These two ideas cut through the bullshit and take you back to the true, authentic self that you will take into the rest of Part Two. They are key to you being able to recognise what is driving your emotions and your thoughts and feelings. By having that awareness, you can then choose how to positively respond in a way that lives up to what you stand for and stops you reacting to the perceptions created by fitting into a mould.

You have to know yourself better than anyone else.

Others

This is where you'll have some fun! You know when you attend that training course and the trainer starts telling you about the same model that the last trainer told you about? Or when they use the same story of some well-known leader or organisation that every other trainer dines out on? Or when another leadership book tells you about the same analogy/fable/quote/experiment/research? Suddenly, you're feeling like you've heard it all before... but you still haven't done anything with it! Well, that ain't going to happen this time. I can guarantee that you'll never have been asked to create your No-Moan Zone or Circle of Nobheads before, and that's what you're going to do in the coming chapters.

Being able to make positive choices and be the leader that you want to be has to be achieved with simple, practical methods so that you can make a difference– for you and those around you. Both your No-Moan Zone and the Circle of Nobheads are simple tools that you can create and continue to review and update. They are a great way to spark a creative conversation with your team. We've all heard of the corporate tools to use for stakeholder management and problem solving, but we've either forgotten them or got bored of them. Maybe you've tried them and found them to fit the mould and be completely useless! You won't forget my tools, because they talk to you in a no-nonsense way– and you can never get bored of removing moaning or keeping life's nobheads at arm's length. These two tools make sure that you create a positive, proactive environment and that you don't waste time and energy on the people who contribute nothing to you being successful and happy as a leader.

Your No-Moan Zone and Circle of Nobheads are tools that you can do for yourself first before introducing them to your team; it always starts with you, but it doesn't end there. Every team in the world needs a No-Moan Zone and also needs to be clear on who the nobheads are who could stop them achieving what they want to achieve. As a leader, when you introduce these two tools to your team it shows them that you are authentic, because you will drop the corporate bullshit and talk to them like the adults they are. Plus, it's much more fun this way! As a leader, you can never, ever underestimate the value of the element of surprise. No one expects you to be equipped with a No-Moan Zone or Circle of Nobheads! I'll show you the practical steps to put these two tools into practice and how important they are to you breaking the mould.

"A mould that we're expected to fit as leaders is to be able to tell people what to do and have all the answers; that's a mould that needs smashing to bits."

You have power over your mind – not outside events. Realise this, and you will find strength.

– MARCUS AURELIUS

In the final two chapters, I am going to introduce you to two habits you can adopt to create the environment where you want to work and where people want you to be their leader:

➡ Habit 1 – Ask, Don't Tell

➡ Habit 2 – LISTEN

The reason I have kept these two habits until last is because they really break the mould. They can have a huge positive impact on your leadership because, while they are both simple to adopt and both are things that everyone is capable of, they are unexpected traits in leaders. A mould that we're expected to fit as leaders is to be able to tell people what to do and have all the answers; that's a mould that needs smashing to bits, never mind just breaking!

These two habits will enable you to have the conversations that matter, creating autonomy and accountability for your team while building the relationships that are needed to create an environment for empowerment where people feel safe to be themselves. Your impact as a leader is felt in the conversations you have, and by adopting the Ask, Don't Tell and LISTEN habits you will get yourself and those around you enthused from your conversations.

I introduce every leader I work with to these two habits because they are simple yet powerful ways to break the mould and be who you want to be. They're simple because everyone has the ability to adopt them, and powerful because very few leaders choose to adopt them despite – or because of? – the impact they have on empowering others. Before I adopted these two habits, I was spending my days micromanaging people and things and working long hours, going home absolutely knackered and bloody miserable. These two habits stop you from thinking that you have to do everything, and stop you taking your job too seriously. They help you to engage with and inspire others to think for themselves, and this leads to the conversations that you actually want to have as a leader.

I don't need all the things you got; I just wanna be who I want.

– PAUL WELLER

Let me remind you of the cost of not breaking the mould

The personal cost

➡ You can't make the right choices in life. It's the difference between flipping your lid in an ice cream queue and being in control of your emotions so that you can achieve a positive outcome.

➡ You will demonstrate a version of you that creates a negative impression, resulting in you ending up spending more time repairing relationships than building them.

➡ You'll be another stressed-out, unhappy manager trying to be something you're not.

➡ The odds of you becoming a dickhead are dramatically increased.

➡ You'll end up being just like everyone else.

The organisational cost

➡ Company culture is bad, because leaders are blissfully unaware of how their attitudes and behaviours impact on others.

➡ Staff turnover is high because of a lack of emotionally intelligent leaders, so people fail to see that they've gone into self-preservation mode and don't develop or encourage anyone around them.

➡ An executive needs exec coaching because they have never stopped to really get to know themselves as they progress, and fail to see that they haven't changed their behaviours since being promoted from their previous roles.

➡ Communication is rubbish, because leaders don't build relationships and they think that sending lots of emails will get a positive message across.

➡ Performance management is crap because leaders don't choose positive emotions before giving feedback.

You can see where I am going with this! So many of the problems above are never properly resolved, because we try to tick a box and train leaders to get themselves out of the problems they have caused. However, they then go straight back into the mould that fits them. The best place to start to solve the leadership problems in an organisation is to break the mould with the most important and effective tool available: *you*. It always starts with you.

You got to make a change; we got to make a change

I know that when *that* person plays up again, or when *those* situations happen again, it can be so easy to react as you always have done, maybe starting to blame others and looking for excuses while losing your shit with your team. Breaking the mould will uncover another path. It might seem like a very narrow path right now, but it's there. Of course, it's up to you how much you practise going down this path versus the one you've always known, but when you choose this path over and over again, your positive responses become automatic. Honestly, what you're about to do is not hard work – fitting the mould and being some-one you're not is much harder!

All of the ideas I am sharing with you have their own ded-icated chapter, but they won't have the impact you want them to have unless you download the *Break the Mould* workbook. If you still haven't downloaded it, then now is the time to do it. It will enrich your learning experience and make sure that you do something with the time and money you have invested in reading this book. The workbook is your guide to working with your team to break the mould together, and it's where you can complete some self-devel-opment activities. If you really want to learn to self-coach to choose a positive response to your thoughts and feelings, before you go any further you should go and get the work-book from **www.italwaysstartswithyou.com**

Take a look in the mirror
And what do you see
Do you see it clearer
Or are you deceived
In what you believe
You're only human after all.

— RAG 'N' BONE MAN

CHAPTER 5

AUTHENTICITY WINS EVERY TIME

Do what you're doin'
Say what you're sayin'
Go where you're goin'
Think what you're thinkin'
Sounds good to me.

– HAPPY MONDAYS

Leaders who have broken the mould

To demonstrate the power of breaking the mould and to help motivate you to do the same, let's meet some of the leaders who have already done it. It's important that you recognise that you are never the only one. For every problem or crisis of confidence you face, there are plenty of other people who have experienced similar things in their own way. The best way to overcome these problems is to break the mould.

There are specific examples for how some of the ideas in the chapters that follow work to get you inspired as you hear about the positive experiences of others. Before you start to break the mould, I want to introduce you to three brave leaders who chose to do it and gained the benefits as a result. Not only were they brave enough to be their true, authentic selves, but they have the bravery to share their stories with you in this book.

Hayley's story: from self-doubt to confidence

To give you a perfect example of how breaking the mould helps you, I want to introduce you to Hayley. Hayley is a senior leader in a large organisation and is one of the world's wonderful people. She lights up every conversation. Yet, when I first met Hayley, she was experiencing a slump in her confidence and was struggling to get out of it. She told me:

- 'My head is chocker.'

- 'I am losing my self-confidence.'

- 'I feel like we're not achieving anything.'

- 'If I carry on like this, I will fail.'

I coached Hayley to choose how she wanted to break the mould. She gained a clear picture of her true authentic self, how she could choose a positive response to her thoughts and feelings, and then how she could build the relationships that she needed with her team, line manager and stakeholders. She took herself from self-doubt and not enjoying her role to being her authentic self, developing her team to take more responsibility, putting herself back in control.

A watershed moment for Hayley was when she presented her new business strategy to the executive board, which she admitted would have been a very negative experience six months earlier. She would have been terrified of second-guessing herself and not being confident in what she was presenting. Hayley even told me that she would have most probably created the strategy and then got her boss to present it instead of her, despite it being her work and her passion. Her previous lack of confidence would have meant she allowed others to take the credit for her work and allowed them to decide what happened as a result.

Stop silencing yourself on behalf of others.

– GARRY TURNER

With her new-found confidence, and having rediscovered herself, the presentation was an outstanding success. Hayley presented as her unapologetically authentic self and confidently responded to any challenges, gaining the board's buy-in to her ideas. It was so successful that the CEO called her afterwards to thank her and congratulate her on how well she had positively influenced him and the rest of the board.

When I asked Hayley where she thought this new self-belief had come from, she told me, 'I don't stand in my own way now.' She added that she had overcome some of the things that were making her confidence suffer by 'changing my attitude towards other people, and I have stopped overthinking what they want. I now work in a way that I know works well, and believe in myself.'

Breaking the mould reminds you that the only thing you are 100% in control of is how you choose to respond to your thoughts and feelings. That's where you'll discover the magic of breaking the mould. It's not another supermodel and it doesn't tell you what you should do;

"Breaking the mould reminds you that the only thing you are 100% in control of is how you choose to respond to your thoughts and feelings."

it empowers you to come up with your own solutions that grow your confidence so you can take responsibility for getting positive results, which makes it feel even better for you and those around you.

Let Hayley tell you for herself:

The coaching I did with Tim helped me to get out of my way! Often, we blame the job, the people we work with, the skills we have (or don't have), what way the wind is blowing– but working with Tim has helped me realise it's in my gift to create a career that's totally right for me. He made me realise how my experiences and values make me act and feel the way I do, and how I can use this awareness to lead my team more effectively and encourage them to achieve their aspirations in a way that's right for them.

**When you come from the 'I', it makes
it more translatable to the 'We'.**

– MATTHEW MCCONAUGHEY

Jack's story: from uncertain identity to 100% authentic self

I worked with Jack when he was promoted to a leadership position for the first time and, at the same time, he became a father for the first time too. Both of these things happened during the Covid-19 pandemic, which left Jack leading a team he had never met face to face and raising a baby daughter in a world where she couldn't meet her family. Even worse, Jack and his partner didn't have access to their support, thanks to various lockdowns and social restrictions.

One of the challenges Jack faced during this time was getting clear on his identity and being able to separate himself from work and family; he was putting on his work head in the same house where his newborn daughter was with his partner. Jack was conflicted as to how he should prioritise his time, and wracked with guilt because he was working instead of being with his daughter, or spending time with his daughter during the day when his team might have needed him.

Working to break the mould, I coached Jack to get clarity on exactly what his identity was, how to be kinder to himself and how to be his true authentic self. When combined, all of that enabled him to lose the guilt and confusion over his identity and choose a positive response to the thoughts and feelings he was experiencing during a time when many, many things were new and very important to him.

In the same situation that Jack faced, many of us become stressed and either neglect our work or become the parent that we don't want to be and deny ourselves the time with our families. That's the easy mould to fit into. As the coaching with Jack progressed and he continued to break the mould, he told me that:

He reminded himself daily of what he stood for and what he was doing well, refusing to be drawn into the challenging emotions that his circumstances triggered for him.

He chose when to work and when to spend time with his baby daughter, sometimes starting early and sometimes working late. However, most importantly, he put himself in control of when he did what, working to always support his team while making himself feel more comfortable in the circumstances, both personally and professionally.

He was the guest on an industry-leading podcast where he observed that he came across as his best version of himself; he achieved that by breaking the mould and 'being 100% Jack.'

Jack says:

Working with Tim helped me to do a number of things. Significantly, the protected time and space allowed me to deliberately slow down and think with clarity. In a world of 'always on' and 'fast-paced' it remains a breath of fresh air and an important practice. It's also allowed me to work deeply through challenges, uncovering the root causes of them where needed. By diving beyond shallow thought, I've put in solid, sustainable change.

We've also worked to distil my values, and this has helped me get closer to my non-negotiables for business and life. Because of all of this, I'm a more self-aware father, leader and person. And I'm looking forward to the rest of the journey.

One of the beautiful things about breaking the mould is that you can do it without even knowing that is what you are doing! It becomes part of your flow. I don't work with coaching clients and leadership groups and say, 'OK, now we're going to break the mould.' I work in a way that always starts with you and asks you to take control. I share inspiration and ideas that you can adopt to break the mould yourself. Things work best for you when they are intuitive, and that's how breaking the mould works for you. I've never had an audience member come up to me after one of my inspirational talks and tell me they were impressed by how I broke the mould of other speakers. What they do tell me is that they love the ideas shared and how they are going to use them. It doesn't matter where you're at; what matters is that you are breaking the mould your way to be your best version of you.

I need to grow into my own skin. Thats all Im asking for. Cause you owe me the truth, win or lose.

– TOM GRENNAN

Sean's story: from apoplectic to serene

Sean is a senior leader in a large public sector organisation who still inspires me to this day by how he committed to his personal development and challenged himself at every step to achieve the positive change he wanted.

Sean and I started his coaching in March 2020, when we met face to face once before the UK went into a coronavirus-induced lockdown, meaning the rest of our coaching sessions were conducted online. The coaching moving online is relevant because one of Sean's biggest challenges as a leader was building relationships with his team. This was something that was already difficult for him when working with his team every day, and now he had to suddenly move to remote working.

Sean's development need for coaching was identified through feedback from his team, who rated Sean's leadership as not being up to scratch for his role and experience. In his own words, Sean felt 'hard done to' by this feedback, and we started his coaching programme with him being very honest that he felt his team needed to do more to work better with him. Sean and I worked together on how he wanted to break the mould over the next 12 months.

We started by giving Sean the opportunity to get to know himself better and focused on raising his self-awareness. This enabled him to be clear on what he stood for – his values, his purpose and his non-negotiables. We explored how he needed to behave to live up to these, and how to put his own high standards into positive action, rather than imposing them negatively on himself and his team. Sean had many 'aha moments', like recognising that his desire to challenge his team's work did not come from being a perfectionist or a micromanager; it came from how much he valued high standards and professionalism. Which is never a bad thing for a leader.

If you're just being yourself, then nothing can touch you, nothing can stop you.

– NOEL GALLAGHER

I then challenged Sean about the conversations he was having with his team. After that, he instigated open and honest conversations with them, sharing his own values and exploring what their personal values were and how they aligned. He asked every member of his team, 'What do you need from me as your leader to always perform at your best?' This meant Sean was able to really understand his team and open up transparent lines of communication. When they faced challenges, he would ask the team questions to prompt them to respond in a way that lived up to their values.

Sean admitted that as a leader he had a habit of not hiding his frustrations very well, and he would react in front of his team to show his displeasure or would simply go into 'tell mode' rather than having two-way conversations. He overcame this by holding team sessions where they each shared their values and agreed that they would hold each other accountable for living up to their values, including Sean.

To keep building on Sean's development from the coaching, I captured verbatim feedback from both his team and key stakeholders. The verbatim feedback was not anonymous and included questions such as, 'Tell me something I don't want to hear,' and focused on Sean's relationship management. This feedback demonstrated the progress that Sean had made and informed him about what those around him wanted from their relationship with him moving forward. Sean commented on his feedback by saying, 'I have gone from apoplectic to serene.'

Throughout the coaching, I gave Sean feedback based on my observations – sometimes it was tough feedback to hear – and he embraced it and took it into his interactions with his team. It always heightened his self-awareness, leading to a huge increase in his self-motivation and ability to demonstrate empathy for himself and his team.

Sean shared what he had achieved at the end of the coaching programme:

- 'I am no longer making their problems my problems.'

- 'We now never leave a conversation without both of us getting what we wanted from it.'

- 'I am able to go into coaching mode when it's appropriate, something I never thought I could do.'

- 'I now spend most of my time listening to my team, and they take responsibility for their own performance and behaviours.'

Sean achieved much better feedback from the next annual engagement survey, and we finished the coaching programme with a very clear plan for his future progression. He achieved all of that without seeing any of his team in person for 12 months!

This is one example of how breaking the mould can take a leader from someone who finds themselves in difficult situations, having difficult conversations, lacking trust in their team and their own self-belief, to one who is confident and who looks forward to going to work every day and leading a team.

A standout for Sean during his journey towards breaking the mould was his realisation that he *could* be his authentic self, while having the impact he wanted to have as a leader and achieving the results he wanted for himself and his team.

I asked Sean to sum up his experience from the coaching we did together:

The coaching I did with Tim helped me to understand fully how my actions, decisions and behaviours really impacted on my team, both collectively and as individuals. I went on a real personal journey during my time working with Tim and, while I was initially working with him in order to achieve a goal in my working life, I ultimately found greater understanding of who I am generally as a person. At times, I even found our work to be quite therapeutic! I have developed stronger, more meaningful relationships with my team members and other colleagues as a result of my work with Tim, and I have done so without needing to compromise my authentic self. I look forward to continuing to see the results of my work with him as I develop further my role as a leader in the years to come.

**Emotional intelligence will get
you further in life than anything else.**

– JIMMY PETRUZZI

So what?

➡ You need to work on you.

➡ You need to put yourself at the heart of your leadership and learn more about you.

➡ Leave the corporate bullshit and buzzword bingo for those who fit the mould.

➡ Breaking the mould makes leadership a positive experience.

➡ Behind the leader is the real person.

➡ Just because you're 'the boss' doesn't mean you're entitled to anything.

Get enthused

➡ How positively do you currently respond in the different situations you face?

➡ How clear are you on what your team needs from you?

➡ How will you get out of your own way?

➡ How can you be '100% you' more often?

➡ What do you want breaking the mould to do for you?

➡ What will happen to you if you don't break the mould?

YOU

You just have to work out what you believe in, who to listen to, and not freak yourself out. Just get on with it!

— DAVID BOWIE

CHAPTER 6

YOUR MAP OF THE WORLD

Whether I'm right or whether I'm wrong
Whether I find a place in this
world or never belong
I gotta be me, I've gotta be me
What else can I be but what I am.

– SAMMY DAVIS JR.

I want to introduce you to the most important action you can take to break the mould and understand the emotional reactions you experience to the world around you. When you understand what triggers your thoughts and feelings, then you can make a positive choice over how to respond with them. That is achieved by creating your Map of the World. Your Map of the World shows you who you really are and in turn informs your emotions and the thoughts and feelings that come from them. We start with your Map of the World because it always starts with you and it informs you how to break the mould.

I have explored the Map of the World with many coaching clients and leaders from across the UK, Europe and the US. It translates into every culture and every organisation because it is about you. Not the job you do or where you work— you as your best version of you. Your Map of the World gives you the ability to choose to be who you want to be. It is the lens through which you see the world and it always starts with you, so you have to make sure that your lens is not what others tell you it should be.

You're made up from what you learn from other people. Your character and ability to build relationships come from what you learn from others. You decide which positive influences become you.

What is your Map of the World?

Your Map of the World is what makes you you. It is your values, your beliefs, your purpose, your principles, your non-negotiables, what makes your heart sing and what pisses you off. Simply put, it is what you stand for and what you stand against. It is all of the positive influences that you are made up of. It is your personality and moral compass all rolled into one. It engages you with yourself by taking you back to the best version of you that you want to present to the world.

Building their Map of the World is one of the first things I do with all my coaching clients and is a central part of the leadership development that I facilitate, because it shows you why you react the way you do to the world around you and demonstrates to you what really motivates you.

Spend all your life just to find out
All that matters is close to you
The people you know
The things that you're shown
That shape our views
The places you've been
To follow a dream.

– PAUL WELLER

I start with this because you first need to know who you really are. If you don't really know who you are and what's important to you, it's very easy for you to get shoved into someone else's mould without even realising it. One day you might wake up and wonder how you got there– or, worse still, you might carry on living life squeezed into that mould without questioning it until it's too late.

Your Map of the World helps you to break the mould, as no employer or job will ever create a mould just for you that fits you perfectly. Your Map of the World is you. When you create your Map of the World and then you lead and behave based on what is on it, you learn to trust yourself as a leader. No matter what happens, you will always respond in a way that lives up to what you stand for. Think of your ideal leader and what you would want from them, and it will align with your Map of the World and your firmly held human values; it represents what you want from others and, therefore, what you expect from yourself first. People who fit the mould haven't created their Map of the World and end up choosing attitudes and behaviours they don't recognise and fail to take accountability for.

"Understanding your emotional reactions is how you enable the single greatest power you have as a human being: your ability to choose how you respond to your thoughts and feelings."

It's a fact of life that where we come from is important. And you come out of there with an identity.

– SIR ALEX FERGUSON

Why is your Map of the World so important?

I explained in Chapter 3 that we are all emotional creatures. What is on your Map of the World is you as that emotional creature; the map shows you what fuels your emotional reactions to the world and dictates your thoughts and feelings and the attitudes and behaviours that come from them. Understanding your emotional reactions is how you enable the single greatest power you have as a human being: your ability to choose how you respond to your thoughts and feelings.

We each have a range of emotional reactions that inform our thoughts and feelings. Whatever you are doing, wherever you are, whoever you are with, your heart and mind are watching and listening to the world around you to identify and determine whether it aligns or conflicts with how you want it to look, sound and feel. Your heart and mind are like your own personal radar system, constantly scanning the world around you for what they perceive to be threats or rewards.

A good way to think of your Map of the World is to imagine you are scrolling through your social media feed. Some posts that pop up make you want to 'like' them and add a positive comment; others make you recoil in disgust or make you angry and you want to tell them what you think of them or, better still, block them from your feed. That's what's happening to you all the time in the real world. Your heart and mind, fuelled by your Map of the World, are scrolling through your emotional 'feed' and telling you what you like and what you want to block.

When your world aligns with how you want it to look, sound and feel, it is perceived as a reward and you experience positive emotions, putting you at ease with your thoughts, so you feel enthused by and confident in what you're experiencing. This makes positive attitudes and behaviours easy to come by.

When the world conflicts with how you want it to look, sound and feel, that conflict is perceived as a threat, which means you experience negative emotions, generating thoughts and feelings that challenge you and make you feel angry, unsure or even frightened. Here is where you have to choose a positive response and not succumb to negative attitudes and behaviours.

It really is that black and white, in terms of how you react emotionally to the world around you. You have your caveman ancestors to thank for this, as they grew up in a world of physical threats and constant misunderstanding of the world and themselves. The primal human brain hasn't moved on that much over the last 60 million years, but the world has. A caveman's negative emotions were triggered by wild predators and other tribes trying to kill him and steal his food and family. Our negative emotions in today's world are commonly triggered by being unsure how to lead people, whether people will like our presentations, or things like imposter syndrome and not getting enough likes on social media. While the causes of negative emotions have changed, our initial emotional reaction hasn't and, to accompany that, our understanding of and need for intrinsic rewards and instant gratification have become even greater, which poses the chance of a negative emotional reaction and thus negative self-talk being even stronger in a seemingly innocuous interaction.

Human beings are the only animal with the ability to have thoughts about our thoughts.

– MARK MANSON

Your Map of the World helps you to see through all the BS about different generations and to see the human being, regardless of their age and background. When you lead from your Map of the World, you're better able to lead all generations, because you can see that it is the world that has changed, not the people in it. People of any age just want a decent human being to lead them. They can take critical feedback and you being direct at the right time when they see it comes from a point of authenticity, and that authenticity starts with your Map of the World – because it always starts with you.

What has it got to do with breaking the mould?

It always starts with you, and your Map of the World plays a key part in that. The moulds you fit come from your perceptions of what others expect of you and the thoughts and feelings that come with them. Getting clear on who you are and what you stand for from your Map of the World informs how you break free from those moulds by helping you to positively respond to your thoughts and feelings. People who break the mould respond to anything that is going on and anything that others say or do from the perspective of their own values and purpose. Your Map of the World is how you respond to narcissistic nobheads: by acting with integrity and choosing not to fit their mould, and by working to achieve your personal purpose. A classic sign of leaders who fit the mould is when they spend their time reacting emotionally to their perceptions, accentuating their negativity by failing to trigger any of their own positive emotive drivers, to which they are oblivious. Your Map of the World means that you will break the mould by leading yourself and others in a value-led way and by overcoming your negative emotions in a way that lives up to what you stand for.

I can only be what God can see.

– PAUL WELLER

How to build your Map of the World

Your Map of the World helps you to recognise what you are experiencing emotionally and takes you beyond the surface level to your inner best version of you, who is always activating your thoughts and feelings. You build it by answering three questions:

1. What do you stand for?

2. What is your purpose?

3. What are your emotive drivers?

I wonder what my soul does all day while I'm at work.

— GRAFFITI IN LONDON

We're going to explore the questions involved to set the scene, and then I invite you to give it a go and take some time to build your Map of the World. See it as a brainstorming activity; be curious about where it takes you and what you learn about yourself from it. There is no right or wrong on your Map of the World, nor has it got anything to do with anyone else, because it is yours. You are a decent human being, so trust yourself that everything on your Map of the World will be appropriate and important to you.

I have taken one for the team by sharing my Map of the World in the workbook as an example to provide some context for you. Reading mine will give you food for thought and encourage you to consider what is on your own Map of the World and the influences that led to those things being there. Also, if you are going to judge this book in any way, then please only judge it against how it aligns with my Map of the World. Don't judge it for whether it wins any prizes or achieves bestseller status, or how it compares to other books you've read. If you are the judging type, then please only judge the book or me based on whether I live up to what is on my Map of the World.

Let's look at each question to unlock your Map of the World.

1. What do you stand for?

This is your values, your beliefs, your principles and your non-negotiables. It determines what you will and won't tolerate from yourself and others. It includes those people who have had a distinct positive influence on you and what you stand for. Your cultural influences play a huge part here, and perhaps personal interests, religion and education also shape some people's Maps of the World.

Write down the names of the people, cultures and experiences that shaped you – consider your upbringing and firmly held values to recognise where your beliefs about the world come from, helping you to understand what drives your responses to the world around you.

When you become clear about what you stand for, it guides your attitudes and how you want to behave. Everything that you stand for is your best version of you. It is your personal brand. It is what you bleed if someone cuts you in half. Knowing what you stand for gives you full accountability for who you are and what you do. It opens your mind to why you react in the way that you do and exposes the real truth behind why you find certain situations and people more challenging than others. Most importantly, it tells you how you want to respond to your thoughts and feelings.

Values are like fingerprints. Nobody's are the same, but you leave them all over everything you do.

– ELVIS PRESLEY

2. What is your purpose?

Why are you here? What is your job on the planet? What is it that you need to do, that you know something about, that won't happen unless you take responsibility for it? Look for your personal purpose, and live life on purpose. No one can impose your purpose on you, and it definitely isn't found on your office wall or company website. When we have a strong personal purpose, we can deal with anything that happens in our mind.

Knowing what your purpose is can be the hardest part of your Map of the World – mainly because no one ever asks you! You might get told what the purpose of your employer is, but very few people get asked about their purpose or are expected to assume one based on the job they do. Your personal purpose is *not* what it says on your job description; it is what you want to get from being a leader and from your life. Get your personal purpose right and then align your professional purpose with that.

The purpose of life is a life of purpose.

– ROBERT BYRNE

3. What are your emotive drivers?

In other words, what makes your heart sing, and what makes you want to die inside? You are at your best when your environment aligns with what is in your heart and mind and at your worst when it feels like everything around you conflicts with who you are and what you stand for. When you get clear on both your positive and negative emotive drivers, you can seek out the work you really want to do and the people you really want to do it with.

Your positive emotive drivers are what inspire you to take action. When you experience them, you want to do positive work with other people. You will feel like you are 'in the zone' and be confident in what you are doing, approaching your tasks and conversations with enthusiasm because you are ready to respond to any challenges that arise.

Your negative emotive drivers make you feel hard done by and trigger behaviours that you don't enjoy – angry exchanges or withdrawing from other people. You will feel like you are not good enough or like others are letting you down and treating you unfairly. Raising your awareness of your negative emotive drivers can be one of the most powerful things you can do as a leader, as it means you will recognise them sooner when they are set off, you can understand what has triggered them and you can choose what happens next.

Don't try to be someone else. The route of emotional intelligence is authenticity, both to yourself and others. Without it, emotional intelligence loses its purpose.

– ILANA ZIVKOVICH

Your one thing to do is your Map of the World

If you choose just one thing to do as a result of reading this book, make sure it is creating your Map of the World. It pays dividends for you in your job satisfaction. Behaving in a way that aligns with what is on your Map of the World is what tells you that you did a good job when your head hits the pillow at night, not completing a task or responding to hundreds of emails. It's that intrinsic feeling of heightened job satisfaction that comes from your heart and mind telling you that today you lived up to being your best version of you and worked with people who demonstrated the attitudes and behaviours that tell you the world is a good place. Your Map of the World reminds you that the one and only thing you are truly accountable for is living up to what you stand for… Every. Single. Day.

Many people take jobs for the package or status and are miserable 12 months later. That's not because they failed at their 'dream job'. It's because the mould they were expected to fit into conflicted with their Map of the World. People who moan about others' behaviour or a perceived injustice aren't moaning because they are negative; it's because what they see, hear and feel conflicts with their Map of the World. When you get clear on your Map of the World, you can choose to stop moaning and recognise that other people's behaviour is their problem and the only thing you can do is choose how to respond in a way that aligns with your own map.

Build your Map of the World using the worksheet in the workbook. The workbook provides a space for you to build your map, and also shares more guidance and examples on what to consider. Go get yours at:

www.italwaysstartswithyou.com

To be yourself in a world that is constantly trying to make you something else is the greatest accomplishment.

– RALPH WALDO EMERSON

Imagine a world where you as a leader can be your true authentic self, your team takes accountability for their behaviours and performance, and you're able to have open, honest conversations. It's not a dream world or utopia; it is possible, and it is achieved by getting clarity on your Map of the World and engaging with your team to understand theirs. I work on this with every leadership team and coaching client I work with, and it is often the part of their development that resonates with them the most as they can relate to it and start to see it at play in their interactions as a leader. This is the start of engaging with yourself and enhancing your self-awareness. With that awareness, everything else becomes easier.

That world is a reality for Enthuse Coaching client Amy. Here's what creating her Map of the World did for her:

"Since Tim introduced me to my Map of the World, everything that I do has been put into perspective. When Tim first took me through it, I knew it would be a great tool as he wouldn't use any old crap. What I didn't realise was quite how great it would be and the impact it would have. It's helped me to really find out what is important to me, but also what great qualities make me... me! It's given me the confidence to stay true to myself, be authentic and embrace some of those 'flaws' that I think I have. It was the perfect tool at the perfect time and really helped to kickstart our coaching relationship."

Once you know what you stand for, the rest gets easier.

– SETH GODIN

How does your Map of the World help you break the mould?

➡ It gives you absolute clarity on who you really are and what you stand for.

➡ It helps you understand your emotional reactions to the world around you.

➡ It informs how you choose to respond to the world around you.

➡ It puts your true, authentic self at the heart of your leadership by choosing your ABCs that align with your Map of the World.

CHAPTER 7

ASK YOURSELF FIRST

**Before you can coach others, you must
first learn to coach yourself.**

– JOHAN CRUYFF

When you have created your Map of the World to raise your awareness of who you are and what you stand for, you can start to put that awareness into action. A default position for us in our heads is to question others or the environment that we work in. What you need to do is start with you and first ask yourself those questions.

What am I talking about? I'm talking about what you say to yourself and how you say it. Your self-talk is the voice inside your head – we all have one! It is how you hear and feel your emotions. Your self-talk will natter away to you

"Getting to know your self-talk and learning to master it is a key part of breaking the mould."

whether you ask it to or not. It is a direct result of the emotional reactions that your heart and mind have to the world around you. It is the thoughts you hear in your head and the thing that determines your attitudes and behaviours.

I want to show you how you can take the opportunity to check in with you and positively influence your self-talk to make sure your attitudes and behaviours align with your Map of the World. This helps you to overcome one of the biggest challenges with fitting the mould. Fitting the mould makes your self-talk become something that goes against your Map of the World. The last thing you want is your self-talk being narrated by what others tell you to be and the perceptions that come with that. When you Ask Yourself First, you write the script for your self-talk and make sure it comes from what you stand for and who you really are at your true, authentic best.

Getting to know your self-talk and learning to master it is a key part of breaking the mould.

You know who's gonna give you everything?... Yourself!

– DIANE VON FURSTENBERG

Why is your self-talk important?

One of the biggest barriers to leaders being their best version of themselves isn't that they don't know how to lead
people or that they haven't got the right experience. It's
because they don't get to know or master their self-talk.
When a leader isn't doing something they're supposed to
do, appears incapable, or lacks the experience to do something, then it gets put down to a lack of skill, and off they
get sent on the latest training course or to do some e-learning. But those skills are redundant if you can't first master
your self-talk. That's what stops so many leaders being who
they want to be and, in turn, creates toxic organisational
cultures.

➡ Your self-talk stops you giving feedback, because it
  tells you it will be a 'difficult conversation'.

➡ Your self-talk stops you from finishing work on time,
  because it tells you that you need to 'look busy' so
  your boss thinks you're doing your job.

➡ Your self-talk stops you from declining meeting
  invites and doing what adds real value to you and
  your team, because it convinces you that 'I need to
  be there or I'll miss out on something'.

➡ Your self-talk stops you delegating to your team,
  because it tells you that 'it's quicker if I do it myself'.

Getting to know your self-talk takes hard work – there are no wimps allowed in self-awareness! I encourage you to write down your answers to the self-coaching questions I will share (there is space to do so in the workbook) so that getting to know your self-talk becomes part of your daily practice. As you practise this, it becomes much more intuitive, and you can recognise your self-talk so you can do the things you want to do as a leader. The hard work you put into getting to know your self-talk means that you can then ask yourself what you want to happen and how you want to feel. This turns your awareness into action as you start to positively influence your self-talk and create your own self-fulfilling prophecy.

Those who never change their minds, never change anything.

– WINSTON CHURCHILL

What has it got to do with breaking the mould?

Your self-talk is how you hear and feel the perceptions that tempt you to fit the mould. If you don't understand it, then you will follow it blindly into a mould created for you by everyone else. The difference between fitting the mould and breaking the mould is to choose not to react to your perceptions and instead to choose a positive response to your thoughts and feelings. Your self-talk is the thing that tells you what your thoughts and feelings are and is, therefore, what you are responding to. When you get to know your self-talk, you recognise and understand your perceptions and then you master your self-talk, so it is always either curated by your true, authentic self or you use it to respond. People who fit the mould never have a good conversation with themselves. They start their day by telling themselves that it will be a bad day. Throughout their days, they repeatedly tell themselves they have too much to do, and they end their days by telling themselves that tomorrow will be exactly the same! When you Ask Yourself First, you are always creating the opportunity to make talking to yourself a positive experience.

How to master your self-talk

1. Get to know your self-talk

To master your self-talk, you first have to get to know it. This is a conscious practice where you reflect on what your self-talk tells you and you raise your self-awareness to recognise whether your self-talk is helpful or not. You can start this with a bigger-picture awareness of your self-talk. Consider the questions below:

➡ What does your self-talk tell you about you? What are your thoughts and feelings regularly saying to you? Is it positive or negative?

➡ Why does your self-talk tell you that? What experiences have you had, or do you regularly have, that influence your self-talk? What perceptions do you have that make your self-talk what it is?

➡ How does your self-talk make you feel? What kind of emotions do you regularly experience as a result of your self-talk? How do you want your self-talk to make you feel?

Just stop and think about those questions and be curious about your consistent self-talk. Sure, it will change as you face different situations, but what's the constant beat to it? What are the recurring thoughts and feelings that you can recognise about yourself?

I am able to control only that which I am aware of. That which I am unaware of controls me. Awareness empowers me.

– SIR JOHN WHITMORE

2. Start the day with you

It's not just your consistent self-talk that gets you engaged with you. Stop and think and pay attention to your self-talk at the start, middle and end of your days. Your self-talk is on as soon as your alarm clock goes off. Many leaders I worked with during the Covid-19 pandemic told me how they found themselves starting their day by having break-fast at their laptop at 7am, just because they no longer needed to travel to the office and thought they needed to use that time to do even more work! No amount of time management training fixes that for them. What does fix it is becoming more aware of their self-talk.

Your self-talk very easily becomes your self-fulfilling proph-ecy; if you regularly tell yourself that you'll have a bad day, then you will have more bad days than good. With aware-ness of your self-talk, you can create your own self-fulfilling prophecy and start to change your consistent self-talk to be something that is helpful to you and encourages you to be your best version of you. Instead of starting the day with social media and your to-do list, stop and ask your-self about how your self-talk is setting you up for the day ahead. At the earliest opportunity in your day, stop and ask:

➡ What is my self-talk telling me about today?

➡ Why is it telling me that?

➡ What is true about today from my self-talk?

➡ How helpful is my self-talk about today?

➡ How is that making me feel about today?

Then master your self-talk by triggering a positive self-fulfilling prophecy; ask yourself:

➡ What will I make happen today?

➡ What will I do to make today a good day?

➡ How will I make others feel today?

➡ Why is today important to me?

Starting your day by raising your awareness makes sure that you won't rush into doing something that adds no value to you or those around you. Those leaders having their cornflakes while reading their emails were doing it in reaction to self-talk telling them that's what was expected of them because they were working from home, or telling them they had to prove to others that they were actually doing something at home just because people couldn't physically see what they were doing. The reality is that when these leaders allow their self-talk to determine their actions, they are knackered by lunchtime and start to create a vicious circle for themselves. Their self-talk starts telling them that everyone else should be working from 7am every morning just because they are, and they even start telling their team to do the same!

Self-awareness, my friend, is the solution.

– THOMAS ERIKSON

3. Check in during your day

During your day can be one of the best times to get to know your self-talk, because your self-talk changes as your emotions change and the in-the-moment experiences you have start to impact on it as the day progresses. Take meetings as an example of how important it is to pay attention to your self-talk. How many meetings have you been to where someone came across like a dickhead or seemed completely disengaged? I've been in meetings where grown men have shouted at each other, and people have even started to cry. I've also seen inappropriate behaviour bordering on bullying at meetings. Sometimes people have fallen asleep. And don't get me started on some of the things people do on Teams calls all day!

Had those people stopped and paid attention to their self-talk before going into the meeting, there is no way they would have heard 'I hope I get really angry and have a massive argument with one of my colleagues' or 'I want to feel like I am not good at my job and cry in front of my peers'. No one ever consciously thinks 'this is the meeting where I will threaten, intimidate and belittle someone because of their team's performance, and come across like a bully' and they definitely wouldn't have thought 'I think I'll use this meeting to get some kip in front of other people'!

Yet those things happen because as we move from meeting to meeting, our emotions build up and we start to change our self-talk so that, by the time we get to the tenth Teams call of the day and boring Barbara is telling us the same thing she tells us every week, our self-talk rapidly gets us into a situation we didn't plan for.

Take time in between your meetings to ask yourself some questions and make sure you are aware of what self-talk you are taking into your next meeting with you:

➡ What is my self-talk telling me about this next meeting?

➡ Why is it telling me that? Is it because of what happened in my last meeting or is it all about how I feel about this one?

➡ How will I make sure that my self-talk doesn't choose how I come across in this meeting?

One of the most important things that many leaders have learnt to do since remote working became more prevalent for them is to block out 10 or 15 minutes in between each of their calls to give them space to breathe – just to stop and think about what is happening for them and make sure they go into their next call with the clear head that comes from engaging with their self-talk.

Use that time before your next meeting to ask yourself:

➡ What do I want to get from this meeting?

➡ How do I want to feel after this meeting?

➡ What do I want other people to get from this meeting with me?

➡ How do I want others to feel after this meeting with me?

➡ What has happened because of me so far today?

➡ What will I do for the rest of the day to be positive?

Using these questions to check in with yourself during your days makes sure that your day doesn't run away from you and that you consistently switch on your self-awareness.

We learn from everything, and a bad thing can be turned into a good thing.

– ERIC CANTONA

4. At the end of the day, all you have is you

Your start to the day and your experiences during it are leading to the end of your day. After one day finishes, another will follow. Ask yourself at the end of every day what your self-talk is telling you about what's happened and what to do next. Engaging with yourself at the end of your days is a great way to make sure you don't join the 'let's just do what we've always done' brigade. Complacency comes from ignoring your self-talk and creates a habit of learning nothing from your experiences but still expecting tomorrow to be different.

Take some time at the end of each day to check in with your self-talk:

➡ What is my self-talk telling me about today?

➡ Why is it telling me that?

➡ How is that making me feel about today and tomorrow?

All you're ever doing is having experiences and learning from them. When you pay attention to your self-talk, you are choosing what you are going to learn from every day, and that awareness puts you in control of what happens in the future. When I would go home from work and be a miserable bastard to my wife and kids, it was because I allowed my self-talk to run away with me and I didn't stop to be aware of what was going on and why. Yes, I had a bad day at work – shit happens, right? Had I got to know my self-talk, I would have recognised that none of it was the fault of my wife and kids and I would have chosen to see that going home and being a dad and husband was the best way to brighten up my self-talk.

The mind is always working. It's supposed to! The trick to life is not to allow that mind to be your master, and to make it your servant.

– HUGH JACKMAN

At the end of your day, reflect on what happened today to shape what your self-talk remembers from your experiences:

➡ How did I live up to what I stand for today?

➡ What impact did I have on myself and others today?

➡ What have I learnt about myself today?

➡ What happened because of me today?

➡ What did I do well today?

➡ What will I do even better tomorrow?

It doesn't matter where you're at; it's where you're going that matters. Put the graft in and better times are inevitable.

– GERRY CINNAMON

A very powerful example of how asking yourself first can help you to break the mould is James, an experienced leader I worked with on an Enthuse Your Leadership programme. It's fair to say that when the programme started, James was a bit of a cantankerous sod, stuck on autopilot, allowing his self-talk to guide everything he did and what happened to him and his team.

As we explored self-talk with the group, James was very open and honest about his and how it shaped his behaviour towards his team, sharing that his self-talk was negative and that it was based on his previous run-ins with people. Those run-ins shaped his self-talk and told him that another run-in was only around the corner, so he behaved in line with that perception, preparing himself for a battle and being defensive and negative. I encouraged James to master his self-talk. I said to him, 'You're going to have run-ins with people as a leader; get over it. What do you want your self-talk to tell you?' My honesty resonated with James, and he spent the majority of the programme getting to know and master his self-talk because he recognised the problems it was causing him.

James practised different questions to turn his self-talk into an empowering commentary for himself and his team. At the end of the programme, he shared an insight from what he learnt:

> I used to sit in an office giving out orders. Saying 'do **this, this,** this and this' to my team and expecting them to do what I told them. I realised that's the worst way to get people's buy-in and it pissed them off rather than getting them to think for themselves. When I mastered my self-talk and led my team in the

way that I really wanted to, I let go of what had hap-
pened in the past and I didn't have to tell them what
to do; they wanted to do it for themselves.

How does Ask Yourself First help you to break the mould?

➡ It allows you to understand your self-talk.

➡ It makes sure you always start with you.

➡ It gives you more good days than bad.

➡ It is how you master your self-talk.

OTHERS

The culture we have does not make people feel good about themselves. And you have to be strong enough to say if the culture doesn't work for you, don't buy it.

– MORRIE SCHWARTZ

CHAPTER 8

YOUR NO-MOAN ZONE

**Human beings want to love their organisa-
tion – they don't want to work for a set of
bastards.**

– JIM MCNEISH

'Will you lot just shut up moaning?'

There is a leader somewhere in every organisation across the world who has either said or wanted to say those words to their team or to their peers. Moaning is like a global pandemic in itself and, if anything, it's getting more widespread as many people spend their mornings or breaks at work scrolling social media, venting their displeasure or moaning to other people about what other people are doing.

The Google dictionary definition of *moan* is to 'complain or grumble, typically about something trivial'.[3] People take up moaning because they think you're not listening to them. If I don't think you're listening to me, then I can say whatever I want without fear of reproach and without having to worry that I'll be held accountable for the thing I'm moaning about. People who fit the mould are the world's greatest moaners. Most great moaners are the ones who say things like 'I know my place' or 'that's the way it is here' and are complete inspiration killers. Your opportunity is to choose not to moan and to not allow it to become part of how you and your team work. Yes, we are all very good at moaning and yes, there are many things we like to moan about; so break the mould by choosing a different response to create a positive environment where time and energy are never wasted on things you can't do anything about. Choosing not to moan sets the tone for how you want people to behave at work and the attitudes they have. No one wants to be the cranky, difficult person when the boss is calm and approachable.

What is a No-Moan Zone?

It's the place where you put away everything that creates negative energy and wastes your time. It's a positive 'zone' where you focus your time and energy on the things that are within your control and don't allow what other people

---

3   https://www.google.com/search?q=moan+definition

do or the challenges you face to become something you discuss in a negative way. No one wants their work to be negative or to make them feel frustrated or like they are restricted by things outside of their control.

You can have a No-Moan Zone for the things that you will never moan about, or you can have ones for specific parts of what you do (e.g., team meetings, projects). In the zone are things that you won't discuss and you won't allow to become part of what you do. It is how you lead your team with a positive mindset, where you choose to accept that there are things you can do nothing about and so you won't bother moaning about them, because it won't change anything.

Creating and working in a No-Moan Zone is a fantastic way to break the mould, because it acts as a way of preventing you from becoming the kind of leader and team that allow other people and things to determine how you behave. The things we moan about come from our perceptions of what is happening or what will happen. Reacting to these perceptions and moaning about them fits you perfectly into the mould that others set for you. Moaning about things is dead easy. But your No-Moan Zone makes sure you work hard to spend your time at work well (remember that you spend more time at work than anywhere else), collaborating with the people you work with to find solutions and create positive energy for you and those around you.

What has it got to do with breaking the mould?

Next time you hear someone moaning, especially about something they can do nothing about, don't judge them for moaning or call them 'a moaner'. Instead, see them for what they are doing: fitting the mould. Moaning is one of the biggest symptoms of fitting the mould. When you fit the mould, you allow yourself to feel trapped and to believe that you can't do anything about it, so you just end up moaning about it, hoping that someone else will change it for you or that your environment will miraculously change. That's never going to happen so, instead, you need to break the mould to change you. When you succumb to moaning, you are fitting the mould because it's the easy option – and, my god, do we humans love an easy option! By resisting the urge to moan, you maintain a positive mindset and start to see that you can spend your time and energy on the things that are within your control. You can choose a positive response to your thoughts and feelings.

Why is a No-Moan Zone important?

Moaning doesn't help anyone. We all think it does and we're all really good at it! It's not getting something off your chest or 'downloading' to get it out of your mind. Nor is it sharing your problem to halve it. It's just fucking moaning! And it doesn't lead to anything positive; no one wants to be the 'Neggy Nelly' or 'Debbie Downer' on the team. You

"Moaning doesn't help anyone. We all think it does and we're all really good at it!"

know the type– the 'mood hoovers' who turn everything into a negative and only ever look at things to find a different perspective they can moan about.

The word that stands out from the definition of moaning above is 'trivial', and the meaning of that is something that is 'of little value or importance'. You need to see moaning in your team as a clear and present danger that needs to be eradicated before it becomes irreversible and seeps into everything that people do.

One of the biggest wastes of time and energy is moaning about the things you can do nothing about – the trivial things. It contributes hugely to people's negative emotions being triggered. It's easy to end up moaning, because there are many things that frustrate us and piss us off, and they feature in our thoughts. Other people's attitudes and behaviours cause us to moan and feel hard done to– especially when they don't live up to our own Map of the World or when we perceive there to be 'one rule for us and one rule for them'. Or the wonderful office politics that become the focus of people's moans: the car parking, the air conditioning, meeting room access, the work fridges and who gets the newer, better laptop/phone/tablet. When I was in one role at an organisation, we used to waste time and energy at the start of every weekly team meeting moaning about how other staff were moaning about the amount of staff discount they got. We were literally sitting there moaning about people moaning!

Leadership happens one conversation at a time.

– SARA BALLINGER

One of the worst traits I have seen in leaders is when they moan about and slag off their team or their peers to other people in the organisation. While everyone is entitled to their opinion, when you choose to openly moan about people, you are setting the tone for both your reputation and for how the people you lead behave. Moaning about other people only reflects on you, not the people you're actually moaning about! And if you moan about things, your team will moan about things; instead of leading towards positive success, you are leading yourself and others in a vicious circle of moaning. You need to practise to preach – no leader ever encourages or wants their staff to spend time moaning, so you need to role model that behaviour. Practising what you preach isn't just about 'getting your hands dirty'; if you want your team to work well with others, then you need to work well with others and not bitch and moan about them and the things they do.

Moaning drains us. It might feel good in the moment to share things and find someone else who feels the same as you– but think about what it feels like after the moaning has finished. You're left with negative energy and an empty feeling brought on by knowing that what you've just spent time and energy moaning about is either something you can do nothing about or something you can't be bothered to do anything about. It helps no one and motivates no one.

**Make your passion stronger
than your fear.**

– NICHOLE MCGILL-HIGGINS

How to create your No-Moan Zone

Your No-Moan Zone creates a positive environment where people can share their frustrations and concerns and the response is always to ask yourself what you can do about those frustrations and concerns. If the answer is nothing, then you let it be and go back to working on what you can do something about. The Beatles had it right: just 'let it be'.

Speaking words of wisdom; let it be.

– THE BEATLES

Creating your No-Moan Zone can be a really fun and engaging thing to do with your team and helps them to get inspired. Everyone knows what moaning looks, sounds and feels like, and no one wants to waste time and energy doing it. Break the mould as a leader and create your No-Moan Zone.

1. Ask them why

The first thing to do to create a No-Moan Zone is to answer the question 'why do you work here?' and remind yourself why you choose to get up every day and go to work where you do. This is a question I ask many groups of leaders. Often, after they have finished telling me all the bad things about where they work and moaned about everyone and everything else, I ask them this question to remind themselves why they choose to go to the place of work they have just been complaining about. This question is often answered with things like:

➡ 'Because I love the people I work with.'

➡ 'I love the work that I do.'

➡ 'I really enjoy helping people.'

➡ 'It's the best place I've ever worked.'

➡ 'I can see that what we do makes a difference to people.'

No one ever tells me that they love going to work every day and moaning or that they like working somewhere that is negative. This tells us what really motivates us to do the work we do with the people we do it with. Of course, the answers to that question bring into sharp focus the question, 'Why the hell are you moaning about it, then?' Ask yourself and your team that question to set the tone for creating your No-Moan Zone. When the moaning starts, go back to that question to motivate each other to overcome the challenges you face.

You can't change your past; you can change your future.

— MARSHALL GOLDSMITH

2. Write a No-Moan Zone list

The next step to creating your No-Moan Zone is to write down all the things that you will not moan about. Be absolutely clear about what would be a waste of your time and energy to moan about. Look for things that are outside of your control and things that won't change. Align it with your Map of the World and commit to never moaning about it. Write down as many things as you can and articulate them in a way that makes sense to you and your time; be specific. Get your team involved and create as big a No-Moan Zone as you can, with everything in there that you have wasted (or could waste) time and energy moaning about. Once you have identified those things that you will not moan about, then agree where moaning will not take place (e.g., one-to-ones, meetings). Remind yourself and your team about this and ask them to take responsibility for making sure no time gets wasted on moaning about the things you can do nothing about.

3. Deal with moans

When moaning does arise, create a set of questions to use to respond to it so that you can decide what needs to be done about it:

➡ Can we do anything about what we're moaning about?

- Yes – stop moaning about it and do something about it.

- No – stop moaning about it and move on.

➡ Will what we're moaning about still be a problem in six months' time?

- Yes – what can we do about it?

- No – let's not moan about it; let's get on with it.

➡ Are we causing the problems that we're moaning about?

- Yes – stop what we're doing to cause the problems.

- No – stop moaning and get on with solving the problems that we *are* causing for ourselves.

By creating your No-Moan Zone and using the questions above, you can turn the environment where you work into a positive one that is focused on being productive, and you and your team can engage in conversations where the focus is to put your time and energy into the things that you can act on. A senior leadership team I worked with on their No-Moan Zone changed their meetings to start with 10 minutes where they all got their moans off their chests and then left them there, focusing the rest of their time together on creating positive change. They only spent time and energy on the things they could do something about.

**Work hard every day on the things that
you can do something about.
Then go to sleep.**

– WINSTON CHURCHILL

Elaine, a senior L&D leader who created her No-Moan Zone after attending an Enthuse Tour event, saw the power of doing this. She shares her experience here of how she used it to break the mould:

*Since Tim introduced me to creating a No-Moan
Zone... I have changed my mindset regarding how
I view my workload and diary commitments. Prior
to this session, I would find myself complaining
about how busy I was, even though some of this was
within my control. Following the session, I flipped
my mindset into a 'No-Moan Zone' and have felt the
benefits from looking at this from a different perspective – no moaning allowed! I have since personally
used this technique on numerous occasions and have*

also discussed it with friends and work colleagues who have introduced this for themselves and in their team meetings. This has helped them to be more effective from an individual perspective and in team meetings. I find Tim's sessions have excellent content; they are always fun and engaging and the 'No-Moan Zone' has helped me immensely.

Use the *Break the Mould* workbook from **www.ital-waysstartswithyou.com** to build your No-Moan Zone with your team and get your No-Moan Zone sign to hold up and stop the moaning. I'd love you to share some pictures with me on social media of you and your teams with your No-Moan Zone signs!

Now your eyes are fixed to the skies
Yet your feet still fixed to the dirt
And I've got this question,
have I got the nerve?

– DOVES

How does your No-Moan Zone help you to break the mould?

➡ It prevents you and others from moaning.

➡ It leads to positive action.

➡ It stops you wasting time and energy on the things you can do nothing about.

➡ It stops you being a moaning sod!

CHAPTER 9

YOUR CIRCLE OF NOBHEADS

What you are

What you need

What you mean for me.

– THE SKYLIGHTS

You're only as strong as the relationships you build

When I first started work and when I was first pro-moted to being a leader, I was never encouraged to work on my relationships. I was told things like:

➡ 'Keep your head down and work hard.'

➡ 'Do as you're told.'

➡ 'Do what they tell you to do and you'll have a job for life.'

➡ 'Make sure your team don't step out of line.'

➡ 'You're the boss now, so you tell them what to do.'

➡ 'If your team don't perform, it's you who I'll come looking for.'

With messages like that ringing in my ears, is it any wonder that I followed the path to fit the mould as a young team member and leader? Only when I started to break the mould and listen to people who saw things differently did I recognise the importance of building value-adding relationships. Then I could clearly see that, whatever you want to achieve, you are only ever as strong as the relationships you build. Luckily for me, that led me to hearing different, much more powerful advice:

➡ 'Whoever you are, whatever you do, wherever you work, you have to be able to rely on other people. And they have to be able to rely on you. You achieve that by building relationships. These are relationships that are strong enough that, when you walk through their door, people want to listen to you and want to help you.'

"Some people will waste your time, and others will fill it with joy."

➡ 'You don't just need relationships with your boss and your team. In every organisation and every role you do, make sure you build relationships with the receptionists, HR, payroll, finance, IT and all the other teams that will impact on you being successful and happy. They will make or break you because, at some point, you will need something from them.'

Some people will waste your time, and others will fill it with joy. The more you work on your relationships, the more your time and energy becomes filled with positivity. Your reputation walks through the door before you do, and how you build your relationships determines what that reputation is and whether people want to be associated with it or not. Leaders who fit the mould think that your success as a leader relies on your technical competence or authority. They live up to the perceptions that every CEO has to be treated like royalty or that HR are to be avoided. They think that they need to have a stronger relationship with their boss than they do with their own team.

Leaders who break the mould recognise that you need strong relationships all over the business and that the ones that contribute the most to you being successful and happy are with the people you have the biggest influence with – your team. They also recognise that you choose your relationships and how much you put into them. Break the mould by developing and relying on your ability to build value-adding relationships and by making positive choices regarding who you spend your time and energy with and how you want to come across to those around you. It's vital to get your relationships right, because the people in your team don't have a relationship with the CEO or with HR. They have a relationship with you, and they want you to break the mould and build value-adding relationships with them.

**You get their behaviours
that you accept.**

– KIRSTY MAC

What is your Circle of Nobheads?

One of the key things to remember to enthuse your relationships is that you always have a choice. You choose who you need to build strong relationships with and who you commit your time and energy to. Some people you will be in constant relationships with, some relationships have a clear purpose and others will come and go. Some are just plain nobheads, and you need to protect your time and energy from them. Your Circle of Nobheads is the place where those people who waste your time and energy are put and kept to make sure that you don't let them get too close to you. People who fit the mould are surrounded and influenced by the nobheads around them.

A nobhead is someone who is an irritating person who is oblivious to how they are perceived. The world is full of them and, if you're not careful, they will take over your time and energy and ruin your other relationships. You are going to build your Circle of Nobheads to protect you from the nobheads you are exposed to and to make sure that you choose to spend your time and energy building relationships with the people who truly matter and who will get you enthused.

I have worked with loads of nobheads. Nobheads who wasted my time writing pointless reports. Nobheads who would always cancel my one-to-ones with them. Nobheads whose incompetence I had to cover up. Nobheads who never listened. Nobheads who made inappropriate comments and told discriminatory jokes. Nobheads who constantly lied. Nobheads who always did what they'd always done. Nobheads who made me feel guilty for taking time off. Nobheads who never gave me any feedback. Nobheads who took the praise for all my hard work. Nobheads who put me in useless meetings and nobheads who sent me on wild goose chases setting up projects that were never going to be approved. I've bought into these nobheads and believed them when they told me they would help me to progress. And then they did nothing for me and left at the first opportunity!

**It is the ability to choose
that makes us human.**

– MADELEINE L'ENGLE

What has it got to do with breaking the mould?

No one chooses to be a nobhead. They become one by fitting the mould, by living up to how others and their environment expect them to behave. Breaking the mould really can be as simple as choosing not to be a nobhead: not to be irritating to others and, more importantly, not to be irritating to yourself. The last thing you want is to be in your team's Circle of Nobheads, or in the wrong circle with your boss or those colleagues who are important to you. Being in the right circle with other people is a result of you choosing a positive response to your thoughts and feelings through mastering your self-talk. Getting your nobheads in the right circle for you is a result of you choosing to demonstrate the attitudes and behaviours that align with your Map of the World so the people around you know that, regardless of how others behave and what they say or do to you, you will choose to spend your time and energy on those who care about you and help you to be successful and happy. When you break the mould, you will not chase the acceptance or approval of people who only care about themselves just because the perception is that kissing their arse or doing what they tell you to do is how you progress. No, you progress by breaking the mould and being your true, authentic self. Only you can decide what real progress actually is for you, and all the nobheads will be just fine without you!

Why is it important to build your Circle of Nobheads?

I could write an entire book on the nobheads who have wasted my time and energy. And, worse still, the nobheads I have allowed to dictate what happened to me at work and how I felt when I went home. You're not going to do that. You are going to move the nobheads as far away from you as possible.

One of the things that makes people fit the mould is that they are oblivious to the nobheads they work with and the things they are allowing said nobheads to do to them. Some leaders think it's OK for their boss to ring them late at night or at the weekend just because 'it's the boss'. That boss is a nobhead who can't organise themselves and so imposes on your life to make them feel better about themselves.

The first important step in creating your Circle of Nobheads is identifying who your nobheads are and why they are nobheads. Then you will choose how to limit the time you spend with them and restrict the power they have over you.

The importance of your Circle of Nobheads is highlighted by how it enables you to see clearly that there is no point expecting or waiting for other people to change. Other people will do whatever they want – once a nobhead, always a nobhead, and all that! When you raise awareness of who your nobheads are, you stop stressing about their behaviour or what they say or do (or don't do). Instead, you focus your time and energy on you. You are the only person who can make you *you*. Most of the nobheads I worked with are still doing the same jobs and probably still showing the same nobhead behaviours. And do you know what? They're absolutely fine. Nothing bad happened to them because I saw them as a nobhead. They are oblivious to it. All the pissing and whining I did about them and all the stress that I allowed them to cause me hasn't changed them in the slightest. But it did change *me*, and for the better. When I put them firmly in my Circle of Nobheads, the stress disappeared and the only person that their behaviour reflected on was them, instead of me going home and moaning about it or chasing my arse trying to do what they told me to do or to clean up their mess.

Creating your Circle of Nobheads is a cathartic and empowering experience. It reminds you that you are not responsible for other people's attitudes and behaviours. You don't need to try to save people or make up for their shortcomings. The importance of it resonates because it makes you focus on you and those who are most important to you.

**We are broken by others,
but we mend ourselves.**

– PAOLO NUTINI

How to build your Circle of Nobheads

1. Draw four concentric circles

You build your Circle of Nobheads by drawing four concentric circles and writing in each one the names of those people with whom you need strong relationships and the nobheads you want to keep away from you. Your first circle is the easiest; it sits at the centre of your universe, and only one name needs to go in it: *you*. You have to put yourself at the centre of your first circle and then build your relationships around you.

Once you have put yourself at the centre of your universe, you can put your relationships into the outer circles. They are:

➡ **Family, friends and colleagues** – this is the circle closest to you. Here you need to put the people you have the most important relationships with – the people who contribute the most to you being happy and successful. Your closest family and friends need to be the first relationships here, as they help you to be your true authentic self and will be there for you whatever happens at work. Then you need to add your most important colleagues. This is where you need to choose. Don't assume that your boss has to be in here, because sometimes they are the biggest nobhead around. If you can put them in here, then fantastic. Same goes for your team: you want them in here, but if they choose to behave in a way that moves them away from you, then so be it. Be brave; be really clear on who you really need to be closest to you, because those people are the ones you are going to commit your time and energy to.

➡ **Positive influence** – this is the most populous circle for many people. It includes the rest of your family and friends, and all of those colleagues and peers with whom you need positive influence. These are the people you need a relationship with and need to be able to rely upon, but do not add the most value to you or hold the key to your happiness and success. This can be the most transient of circles, as sometimes you have to move people in and out of it; some of them become part of your closest circle, and others become nobheads.

➡ **Nobheads** – here they are: the irritating people who are oblivious to how they come across. In this circle you need all the nobheads in your life and work. Think hard about who you need to remove yourself from and stop giving your time and energy to. Some of your family and friends might be nobheads; some of your work colleagues and peers definitely will be! Make sure that you get absolutely clear on who those people are who leave you bad experiences and are only interested in themselves, not you.

2. Now you get to choose

Once you have your circles, then you choose who to spend your time and energy with. You can move people around these circles as your relationships need to change. Don't ever feel guilty about which circle you put people in. You are not judging them or condemning them to a life of nobheadness; you are simply choosing who is most important to you and who needs your time and energy. Your team appreciates you doing this, as the last thing they want is you letting all the nobheads into their world and having their time and energy wasted.

If you have a choice between disappointing yourself or disappointing others... you should get busy disappointing others.

— GLENNON DOYLE

When you have your circles created, you can choose outcomes for the nobheads. Look at your circles and consider who you need to give feedback to, whose meeting invites you need to decline, who you need to build relationships with and who you simply need to let go of and ignore.

Remember that this is you creating powerful relationships that benefit you and your team. It enables you to be your best version of you. People who fit the mould allow the nobheads to decide what happens; people who break the mould are happy and successful because they decide what happens. The people who go home from work and moan about the same things over and over and then get up and do the same thing tomorrow and moan about it all over again are the ones who are allowing the nobheads to choose for them. Choose to spend your time and energy with those who create reciprocal positive influence, so you go home from work knowing that you build strong relationships and behave in a way that lives up to what you stand for.

The Circle of Nobheads is one of my favourite activities to do with coaching clients and leadership teams, and it never fails to make an impact. I worked on this with Faye, a senior HR leader who was frustrated and stressed by the nobheads that she was working with and who were depleting her energy. We spent six months working together, which started with Faye building her Circle of Nobheads and working to change her relationships. At the end of her coaching programme, Faye shared with me:

I can't believe how much of my time was being wasted on my nobheads. I thought I had to impress them and do whatever they told me to do. By building my Circle of Nobheads, I realised that I was sacrificing my most important relationships to try and please the people who are and always will be blockers to my ideas. Once I had identified who my nobheads are and how I wanted to work, I empowered myself to pull away from them and improve the relationships with my team and the people who actually contribute to me being who I want to be.

Build your Circle of Nobheads by using the template in the *Break the Mould* workbook. Get yours here: **www.italwaysstartswithyou.com**.

When you want something to happen, you have to make it happen.

How does your Circle of Nobheads help you break the mould?

➡ It keeps the nobheads at bay.

➡ It means your time is spent with people who help you to be successful and happy.

➡ You build value-adding relationships that you want to be part of.

➡ It stops you becoming someone else's nobhead.

CHAPTER 10

YOUR ASK, DON'T TELL HABIT

Ask questions for which you have no answer.

– JUDITH GLASER

How was work?

This is the ubiquitous question that gets asked around the globe. We get asked it by our parents, our partners, our friends and our children. It may have some different articulations such as 'How was your day?' or 'How did today go?'. Whichever way it gets asked, you can be sure that the people you lead will be getting asked that question regularly. And you have a huge impact on the response that question gets from them.

Stop and think about that now: when the people you lead and the people you work with get asked about their day, what do you want them to say? What can you do to make their response a positive one? The best way to have a positive impact on their days at work is to create an environment where people can think for themselves and where they feel trusted.

Without people, you're nothing.

– JOE STRUMMER

What is Ask, Don't Tell?

It is a habit of asking people powerful open questions that show your genuine interest in empathising with their perspectives and enable you to choose a positive response by truly understanding what's really going on for them. Leaders who fit the mould think they have to always tell people what to do and be the one with all the answers. Team members who fit the mould simply do what they're told with zero accountability. When you adopt the Ask, Don't Tell habit, you create opportunities for people to break the mould, come up with their own solutions and take accountability for their behaviour and performance.

No conversation; no relationship.
No relationship; no conversation.

– STEVE NESTOR

What has it got to do with breaking the mould?

While people want to have a two-way conversation with you, their perceptions tell them that because you are their leader, you will simply tell them what to do, assume authority and bark orders at them. Indeed, millions of people who fit the mould do so because that has been their experience, either as a leader themselves or with other leaders, for many years. When you ask people thought-provoking questions, you instantly break the mould by showing them that you will not always simply tell them what to do and instead will take a genuine interest in them and help them to empower themselves. The most inspirational leaders we

"Knowledge is only truly powerful when it is shared, and when you lead with an Ask, Don't Tell habit, you create an environment where people are expected to think for themselves."

have all worked with will include those who helped you to do things for yourself, do things for the first time, get out of your comfort zone, challenge yourself and believe in yourself. So much of what those leaders do is through the questions they ask. You don't want people to be submissive to you, because then you will have to do all their thinking for them. You want to work in partnership with your team, and for them to take responsibility for their own behaviours and performance. That is achieved by asking them powerful open questions to engage with them and ignite their passion for what they do.

Why is it important?

To highlight the value of this habit, think about what happens to people's motivation and capabilities when they are always told what to do. Constantly telling people what to do and giving them the answers results in them being given the best excuse to stop thinking for themselves. Indeed, they think or feel some or all of the following:

➡ Demotivated – 'Why think for myself when you'll tell me what to do anyway?'

➡ They make their problems your problems – 'You told me to do that.'

➡ No need to take accountability – 'I'll just do what I'm told to do.'

➡ What's the point in doing anything new or different? – 'I'll do what I've always done.'

Some of the attitudes above are inherent in many organisations, and so many of them can be traced back to the leader fitting the mould of thinking they need to have control over everything and be the expert with all the answers. Leaders who fit the mould spout the old 'knowledge is power' bullshit. Knowledge is only truly powerful when it is shared, and when you lead with an Ask, Don't Tell habit, you create an environment where people are expected to think for themselves and you can get on with leading them to high performance instead of being stuck doing all the day-to-day work that they are supposed to be doing!

Just think:
questions, questions, questions.

– SUSAN SCOTT

You can't help other people to change their behaviour by constantly telling them what to do. You have to show them that you want them to change, and make them feel like you want them to change. This is achieved by asking powerful open questions at the right opportunity. Before we go any further with this, I need to point out that this habit is not about answering a question with a question; nor is it about everybody becoming a professional coach. It is about creating an environment where your team know that you expect them to think for themselves, that you want them to choose their own solutions, and that you want to have genuine, meaningful two-way conversations with them. Being part of a team – and the leader is a massive part of the team – you can only control your own performance and what you do. When you choose an Ask, Don't Tell habit, you are putting people in control of their own performance and what they do. That's how you enhance engagement and productivity, not by telling them what to do all the time!

Your job as a leader isn't to tell people what to do; it's to make them believe in themselves.

An Ask, Don't Tell habit sees you put into practice one of the greatest tools at your disposal: asking powerful open questions. By this, I mean:

➡ **What?** Get them thinking by asking 'what' questions. All those 'can you', 'did you' and 'will you' closed and leading questions that proliferate in leaders' vocabulary need to be ditched to help you better understand what is going on for your team and what they think they should do next. Asking 'what do you think?' must be something you consider doing on a daily basis.

➡ **How?** This is the most empowering of questions, because it shows you believe in their ability to find a 'how' for the challenges and problems they face. Imagine how much more confident your team will be when, instead of being told how to do something, you ask them 'how will you resolve that?'

➡ **Why?** This can be the most liberating of questions when you practise using it to its potential. Many people expect a 'why' question to lead to accusations or make them look back at mistakes with regret and shame. Yes, this one takes more practice, and you have to learn to avoid raising barriers – but done well, it sparks a fire in the belly of your team. You demonstrate your own wider thinking and encourage others to do the same when you ask 'why is this important for our customers?' or 'why do you think we've never done anything different before?'

'What', 'how' and 'why' are the only truly powerful open questions you need as a leader. A closed question is either answered with 'yes' or 'no' or is a 'which', 'who', 'when' or 'where' question that merely points to facts, not ideas. I ask leaders, 'What do you do that hinders rather than helps your conversations?' and this leads us to seeing that they don't ask enough powerful open questions. This is often because they think they have to do more of the talking because they're the boss. Asking more questions means you can say less in your conversations. People actually enjoy conversations more when you say less, because it switches your brain on to understanding, and it gives you the new experience of seeing things from somebody else's point of view instead of repeating what you already know.

We're going to look at specific opportunities to introduce an Ask, Don't Tell approach and look at some questions that you can use straight away; these will help you to build your own question library to fuel your Ask, Don't Tell habit. A question library might not be the sexiest thing you'll ever create but it will be one of the best things you'll do, as it gives you the reminder that you can and will ask powerful open questions. Grab a *Break the Mould* workbook from **www.italwaysstartswithyou.com** to see more questions to get you started and to inspire you to build your own powerful question library.

The gift of leadership is helping others to learn more about themselves.

How to use Ask, Don't Tell

You have the opportunity every day to demonstrate an Ask, Don't Tell habit. I have identified some classic examples of what you do as a leader, to show when you can ask powerful questions instead of simply telling people what to do. Use these to try it out and practise it and to inspire you to choose your own opportunities to start asking powerful open questions.

1. In the moment

Your spontaneous conversations are a golden opportunity to demonstrate your Ask, Don't Tell habit. This is where people expect you simply to tell them what to do, or even to do it for them, and it can provide the most frequent opportunities to help people to think for themselves. When you get asked questions by your team, or things get escalated to you, take the opportunity to ask:

➡ What do you think you should do?

➡ How can I help you to resolve this?

➡ What support do you need from me?

➡ What do you want to happen next?

➡ When this has happened before, what did you do?

These questions are not about deflecting responsibility or becoming like a politician who never actually answers questions; they're about helping your team to help themselves and choose their own solution. There is a time and place to tell people what to do. When you adopt an Ask, Don't Tell habit, you become adept at choosing the right time to tell and the right time to ask. Take a global pandemic as a prime example. In March 2020, people needed their leaders to tell them what to do to work safely. Then, in April, they needed to be asked 'How are you?' and 'What support do you need from me?' The two can go hand in hand; the key is choosing to ask first as a habit so you can create engagement and self-motivation in your team.

People are much more motivated to do something when it is their own idea, compared with when other people tell them what to do. Use an Ask, Don't Tell habit so that people can come up with their own solutions in the moment.

2. *To build trust*

Don't miss your opportunity to build trust with your team by using Ask, Don't Tell. Trust is something that is massively important to all of us. High-performing teams are built on a foundation of trust. Yet trust is something that we often just expect to be built, and we each take a different approach to it. I'll trust you until you give me a reason not to, whereas many leaders I've worked for wanted me to earn their trust. Neither is right or wrong or better or worse, but when it isn't talked about then we can be left guessing as to whether trust really exists, and we can be left disappointed and frustrated when people don't trust us in the same way as we trust them.

To build trust with your team: Ask, Don't Tell. One of the simplest yet most impactful things you can do as a leader is to ask your team, 'What do I need to do to build trust with you?' and set out a positive intent by asking, 'How will we know when we trust each other?' And even explore what should happen if trust is lacking: 'What might I do to break trust with you?' and, 'If I don't feel like we trust each other enough, how should I approach that with you?' This shows that you are willing to have the conversations that matter, and you are inviting your team to engage with you to talk about what needs to be talked about.

Trust doesn't get built by sharing business updates and telling people they need to earn your trust; it comes from engaging in a two-way conversation to truly understand what needs to be done to build trust with your team. When you do the things that build trust with your team, they recognise that and are motivated to work even harder for you and the team.

3. In your meetings

How many people do you think are going to meetings every day even though they'd rather be anywhere else? It's commonplace for organisations to have meetings about meetings as a regular occurrence in the lives of their leaders! Or the other classic dead loss meetings are the weekly updates where people gather to tell each other what they did last week and what they're doing this week. Eat. Sleep. Meet. Repeat. When somebody suggests a better approach could be taken, the agenda gets updated, some new slides are created and nothing actually changes.

Make your meetings what they are supposed to be: a coming together of people to create solutions and engage with each other by asking powerful open questions. Think of the meetings you chair regularly and ask yourself, 'What is the purpose of this meeting?' Ask everyone you invite to them, 'What do you want to get from this meeting?' to create meaningful dialogue that makes your meetings worth attending. At the end of each of your meetings, don't ask for minutes or whether anyone has any other business; ask, 'What are we all going to do as a result of this meeting?' to create accountability and motivate people to have something to show for the time they have given up in order to attend your meeting.

Meetings shouldn't be a series of monologues as people take turns to present their updates or opinions; they should be engaging two-way conversations that get people enthused and lead to positive action. A leader I have worked with from a large well-known UK brand was bemoaning the fact that their meetings do not work as well as they expect and blamed their team for this, exclaiming, 'I've asked them to share their ideas loads of times and no one ever has any.' This is representative of what happens when we have a bad conversation: we blame the other person or people involved. Use an Ask, Don't Tell habit to change your perspective at your meetings and think like that leader did when I asked them, 'How can you change the way you ask?' This enabled them to realise that they weren't actually asking for ideas – they were just repeating an agenda point that asked 'does anyone have any new ideas?' which only requires a 'yes' or 'no' response. They changed this to asking, 'What ideas do you want to share?' which got people talking because it had a positive intent and didn't allow for a one-word answer. Sometimes, all it takes is a simple shift to a powerful open question to create real engagement with your team.

Any Other Bullshit

One of the big problems with meetings is that they are a breeding ground for bullshit. They're a great place to play buzzword bingo and spot the one-liners that people use instead of asking powerful open questions. Most meetings include 'any other business' on the agenda, and it's a time when everyone looks around blankly or the same people raise the same issues time and time again. Make AOB stand for Any Other Bullshit and instead of fitting the mould with corporate catchphrases, break the mould with an Ask, Don't Tell habit:

ANY OTHER BULLSHIT	ASK, DON'T TELL
'Let's look at this through a different lens'	What else can we do?
'Think outside the box'	What can we do that we haven't done before?
'Let's touch base and check in on this'	How will we know this is working?
'We need to make this business as usual'	How will we get everyone to do this?
'We must work smart on this'	What will we do if this goes wrong?
'Reach out'	What support do you need?
'We need to hit the ground running'	What is the first thing we need to do?

'Go the extra mile'	Why is this important to you?
'Circle back'	What will actually happen if we don't do this?
'As per my email'	What do you think of my ideas?

When you chair your meetings with an Ask, Don't Tell approach, people will actually want to attend and will also know that it's not another chance to doze off or do their emails while on a video call with you. People who allow their meetings to become slanging matches do it because they think they have to use them as a chance to tell people what to do. Ask people what they think so your meetings become something that engages people and actually leads to things being done as a result. Adopt an Ask, Don't Tell habit to make sure your meetings are not the ones where people talk but don't actually really say anything!

The world is changed by your example, not your opinion.

– PAOLO COELHO

4. In one-to-ones and when giving feedback

These are two of the greatest privileges you get as a leader – they're a chance to engage in two-way conversations and to give people feedback on their behaviours and performance. Let's look at each one.

We'll start with your one-to-one interactions with your team. These are the sacred conversations for you as a leader. They offer the chance for you to really get to know your team and create an environment for empowerment. A cardinal sin for a leader is to cancel or fail to turn up at a one-to-one conversation you planned to have with a team member. The worst managers I worked with were the ones who left you hanging waiting for your one-to-one; it can be soul-destroying to think your boss doesn't have the time or inclination to look you in the eye and engage in a meaningful conversation about you and your work.

You shouldn't be waiting for a performance management process to tell you when to have one-to-ones and what to discuss; your team should tell you what they want to discuss and what they need from their one-to-ones. If the conversation is about their behaviour and performance, then they should lead on the conversation, and your job is to ask powerful open questions to help them think positively and come up with their own solutions.

Consider these questions for your one-to-ones:

➡ What do you want to get from your one-to-ones?

➡ What do you need from me in your one-to-ones?

➡ How can we make sure you get to talk about what you want to talk about at your one-to-ones?

➡ How can I support you?

➡ What do you want to happen at your one-to-ones?

➡ How do you want to feel after your one-to-ones?

➡ Why are your one-to-ones important to you?

➡ What are you going to do as a result of your one-to-ones?

Make sure that your one-to-ones with your team are a place where you provoke thought from them and that you accept your role is to help them to take accountability for themselves. That is achieved by asking them powerful open questions, not by telling them what you think or what they should do.

We have to accept that of course there are things you need to tell them in their one-to-ones – giving feedback, for example, or sharing business goals and strategy to inform their individual goals. As part of your preparation, create a 'tell list' (i.e., your feedback on what they are doing well and what they could improve on) and an 'ask list' (i.e., what goals do they want to achieve and what personal development do they need) to be clear on what you want them to decide for themselves and what input you need to give to guide the questions you will ask them. This helps you to get the balance right and avoid making it feel like an interrogation – and, more importantly, avoid making it feel like it's your one-to-one and not theirs!

When it comes to giving feedback, you need to remember that people don't do what you tell them to do – they do what they tell themselves to do. With that in mind, the best way to give feedback is to ask them powerful open questions so they give the feedback to themselves. Taking an Ask, Don't Tell approach to giving feedback means that your feedback lands, because it is given with their permission, and you show that you are interested in understanding their perspective. In this way, your feedback becomes more honest as it speaks to their DNA instead of feeling like it is being given based on your own agenda.

Let's use an example to bring this to life. You need to give your team some feedback on their behaviours at a meeting with some of their peers. Their behaviour came across as negative, and they did not show the attitude you expect of them (and, most importantly, the one you know they expect from themselves). Instead of piling straight in and telling them what you think and what they should do next time, take an Ask, Don't Tell approach:

➡ Firstly, ask if you can give them some feedback on the specific meeting and how they came across.

Then ask, 'How was the meeting for you?' and, 'How did you want to come across in the meeting?' This might be followed up with, 'How do you think you actually came across?'

➡ Now share your feedback, including specific examples of what you saw from their attitudes and behaviour at the meeting and how that came across to others. Then ask, 'What will you do differently next time?' and, 'How can you make sure that you always come across how you want to come across?' to get them thinking about their own ideas for how to change their behaviour. This shows that you trust them to make the change for themselves.

➡ Close the feedback by asking, 'What are you going to do as a result of my feedback?' and, 'How can I help you after today?' This will gain their commitment to making a change and will show them that you want to continue the conversation.

Take the next opportunity to change the way you give feedback into an Ask, Don't Tell approach and see the difference it makes, both to you and to your team. Yes, OK– the above is an example in a book and it makes it sound easy and, of course, in the real world, you don't know how people will respond so you can't prescribe which questions to ask in each situation. What we're doing here is creating a habit, and giving feedback is a great way to demonstrate to your team that you will ask them powerful open questions to make them think and to give them the chance to decide for themselves how they will learn and improve from working with you.

There is only one way to truly find out what your team needs from you as their leader – ask them!

5. Working collaboratively

This is the leadership classic case of 'It's not rocket science, is it?'! As a leader, you are always expected to work collaboratively with your peers, colleagues and suppliers. Yet this is one of the areas many leaders find difficult, and which many organisations get horribly wrong. For them, collaborative working becomes much more about 'I want this' and 'you need to do that', which erodes trust and breaks relationships as a blame culture replaces the culture of collaboration that all organisations are desperate for.

Take your Ask, Don't Tell habit into working collaboratively by asking people, 'How can I help you?' Set the tone for how you will work together by asking, 'What do you need from me to make sure this goes well?' People who really embrace the Ask, Don't Tell habit go even further and ask, 'What are we going to do if things go wrong?' to set the scene for how they will respond to mistakes being made.

Think about who you are expected to work collaboratively with, and consider what questions you can ask them
to make it work well for you and everyone else involved.
People are happy to blame others and moan about how
people don't work collaboratively with them. Break the
mould by being the leader who asks powerful open questions to make working collaboratively a reality.

6. When recruiting

Interviewing and inducting new starters into your team is
where your Ask, Don't Tell habit can start, and it sets the
tone for the environment in which you and your team work.
Ditch the boring, bog-standard bullshit interview questions
like 'Where do you see yourself in five years?' and instead
ask powerful open questions to spark thought in your
potential new team members:

➡ Why is getting *this* job important to you?

➡ How will I know if you're happy in this job?

➡ What will you do to be engaged with the team and
your work in this role?

➡ What does your current/previous leader do that you
would want me to do or not do?

➡ How will you make sure you feel confident in this
role?

Asking those kinds of questions can add a little bit of fun to the interview as you discover more about your potential recruits, and it allows you to see how well they think when asked powerful open questions. In addition, they are the kind of questions that people can't prepare to answer (not unless they know you have read this book, anyway!), so you can learn how they respond to being asked thought-provoking questions.

Once they have joined the team, engage in regular catch-ups and ask them questions that create honest, open conversations to set the tone for how you want them to work with you:

➡ What has worked well for you so far and what do we need to do to make it even better?

➡ How have you built connections with your colleagues so far?

➡ Why is what we do as a team important to our customers?

➡ What do you think we need to do differently?

These kinds of conversations are never intended to be a test for your team; you are merely creating conversations that make them think. You are showing that you have an Ask, Don't Tell habit and you want them to think for themselves. They then take that into their interactions and, when faced with a challenge, instead of simply passing the buck to you or expecting others to solve things for them, they think for themselves and take responsibility for using their initiative. It is not just in your conversations that your Ask, Don't Tell habit pays dividends for you as a leader; it also stirs a positive, can-do attitude and mindset in your team.

If your team thinks you will give them all the answers, they will respond to challenges with the classic 'I'll have to speak to my manager'. When you show them that you want them to think for themselves, they will do just that and resolve their issues for themselves.

If you always tell people what to do, you are teaching them not to think for themselves.

It's never too late to adopt an Ask, Don't Tell habit. You don't have to wait to ask your new team members or take over a new team to demonstrate this. Start today and ask your team powerful open questions – it can be a great way to re-establish your existing relationships. As a leader, never underestimate the value of the element of surprise; a well-placed, well-intentioned question can be the most powerful, positive surprise you can give to someone. When you lead with an Ask, Don't Tell approach, your team starts to ask you questions and show a genuine interest in you. Leaders who tell people what to do all the time appear unapproachable. Leaders who Ask, Don't Tell are the approachable leaders we all want to be.

How does your Ask, Don't Tell habit help you break the mould?

➡ It enables you to ask powerful open questions.

➡ It creates an environment where you and those around you want to work.

➡ It gets you enthused about your conversations.

CHAPTER 11

YOUR LISTENING HABIT

**The other person's quality of thinking
depends on our quality of listening.**

– NANCY KLINE

I have purposely left this idea for how you can break the mould until last because it is the most underrated, undervalued and least practised habit that leaders have. Accordingly, it is the only one that gets written in capitals. Not because it is some contrived acronym, but because LIS-TENING is fundamental in regard to how you break the mould and become your best version of you.

Honestly, how good are you at listening– *really* listening? And how often do you stop and really listen to your team?

Despite us all having the ability to listen, it's very easy to choose not to. We choose to allow ourselves to be distracted and to think that we only need to listen to come up with our reply. Yet being listened to is up there with the basic human needs like air, water and Wi-Fi. The crying baby wants to be listened to. The toddler having a tantrum in the shop wants to be listened to. The rebellious teenager wants to be listened to. The aspirational young leader wants to be listened to. The middle-aged CEO wants to be listened to. The lonely old person wants to be listened to. That's what we all want – to be listened to. It's one of the best-unkept secrets of the world. When you choose to listen to your team, you break the mould and build relationships that you all get enthused about.

Listening is not a skill. It's a choice.

People who fit the mould don't listen, because they only hear what they want to hear. They choose to listen only to form their own response, not an understanding. This is because their perception of themselves is that they should have the answers and a positive intent to show they're listening by sharing their opinions/experiences. Break the mould by listening to understand. By really LISTENING. By not reacting to your perceptions and instead responding to your thoughts and feelings.

What is *LISTENING?*

It is the most basic human need and the most powerful way to positively influence someone. What everyone expects of you as a leader is that you will listen to them. And I mean really listen. Not make people talk to the back of your head like I used to. And I definitely don't mean still looking at your phone while someone is talking to you. It's easy to think that we're listening when, in fact, we're just nodding away as someone else talks and all we're doing is listening to find a way to justify the response we're going to give or to share our opinions and experiences.

LISTENING is when you give someone your whole attention and you are fully present in the conversation. It is not multitasking or sending emails and catching up on your admin while you are on a Zoom call. LISTENING is the hardest communication skill to master, yet it is how you truly understand someone and what they need from you. You never, ever 100% know what someone else is thinking, so the only way to choose a positive response to what they are thinking is to listen to what they tell you. LISTENING is also key to saving your time, by avoiding the need to repeat conversations because you didn't listen to them properly in the first place.

Most importantly, LISTENING is not a skill; it is a choice. Everyone has the ability to listen, but you have to choose to do it. Choose to switch off your phone and remove any distractions. Choose to listen to what is *not* being said, by observing people's body language and tone of voice. Choose to empathise with people's challenges and not just tell them how to fix things. Choose to allow your thoughts and feelings to pass, and focus on the person in front of you. If you are having a conversation with someone, it has to be the single most important thing you are doing; nothing else in the world can be more important at that moment– otherwise, why are you having the conversation? LISTENING to the other person is the way to show them that they are important to you and that you give a shit about them and what they have to say to you.

What has it got to do with breaking the mould?

Stop listening to your team and see what happens! Your conversations will be boring, they will be exhausting for you, and you will face challenges to every decision you make. We fit the mould and stop listening because we think we've got too much to do or that we haven't got time. Break the mould and show your team that you will really listen to them, and you will experience what leadership is meant to feel like – liberating and empowering, for both you and those around you. Write down the names of the worst leaders you have worked with, or famous examples of dickhead leaders, and you will see a list of people who choose not to listen. They fit the mould because they think the world doesn't expect them to listen or because it makes them soft!

Yet the entire world expects you to listen to them, and it is the key to building trust and rapport.

Why *LISTENING* is important

If you don't yet believe how important it is to listen, remind yourself how frustrating it is when you are talking to someone and you know they are not listening to you. They are choosing selective hearing and demonstrate it by not making eye contact, by looking at their phone, by responding to you with something that shows zero interest in what you just said. They might even take the conversation on to a different topic... or to absolutely nowhere, as they blatantly haven't listened to a bloody word you just said. Really pisses you off, right? So, why would anyone choose not to listen? This innate habit that so many people now have of being in a conversation while staring at their screen screams to you that they have something more important going on than what you are talking to them about. When you are guilty of this, it kills your reputation and your relationship.

If you want to be a leader that no one likes, no one respects, no one trusts and no one wants to work with, then skip this chapter; keep fitting the mould and don't listen to your team.

Break the mould by being enthusiastic about listening to your team; by wanting to know what is going on for them; by remembering that there is always something new to find out. How can you ever make a decision or give people

"*LISTENING breaks the mould because the world tells us not to listen.*"

feedback if you're not listening to them? How can you ever know what your team needs from you if you're not listening to them? How can you ever know what people are really thinking and feeling if you're not listening to them? Leaders who fit the mould tell themselves they know everything and that they've heard it all before. They are then surprised or disappointed when people hand their notice in or when people choose not to buy in to their leadership. Choosing to listen is how you show your true, authentic self and create positive influence with you and those around you.

LISTENING breaks the mould because the world tells us not to listen. Social media takes up our attention. Our phones constantly send us notifications. We get more emails and messages than ever before. We have all the information we need at the touch of a button, and everything happens faster, so we expect our conversations to be the same. Yet all of those things are barriers to listening only when you choose to allow them to get in the way.

Yes, listening is harder than it ever has been, but the challenge is the opportunity. That should motivate you to listen even more. It shows the value of it and gives you the opportunity to stand out as a leader by choosing to listen. It's a choice you can make every day to break the mould.

When you're creating your own reality, it's pretty easy to ignore the facts.

I could have filled a whole chapter with the benefits it brings to you and your team when you choose to really listen. Let's look at some of them: ones I gained and some that I have seen my coaching clients gain from really listening:

➡ It makes your conversations much more cathartic; doing all the talking comes with much more pressure than doing more listening!

➡ You get to really know your team and what they are thinking; you can't get to know people if you never shut up.

➡ It saves you a lot of time; really listening in the first place means that a problem or concern only needs to be aired once. The leaders who are doing too much are the ones who listen the least.

➡ It builds trust; people really believe in what they tell themselves. When you really listen to them, you become the leader they trust. Your listening shows that you want them to listen to themselves and that you trust them to tell themselves the right thing.

➡ You can see things from another's perspective; that's how we learn more about the world in which we live and it empowers you to be more open-minded and non-judgemental. Those are, after all, two traits at the very top of the list of what people expect from leaders.

➡ It builds relationships; nothing else comes close to really listening when it comes to building rapport. Your reputation and job title don't build relationships, but your ability to really listen does.

If you only ever look at things from your own point of view, you'll never learn anything new.

How to LISTEN

1. Choose to LISTEN

LISTENING isn't just about being in the moment and involved in the conversations you have; nor is it exclusive to the skills you can develop or the practical things you can do to really listen. It always starts with you, and the first step is choosing to listen. To make this choice, you need to remind yourself why you will really listen to your team. Answer the questions below to help you to choose to listen:

➡ Why is really listening to people important to me and my team?

➡ How will it help me to really listen to people?

➡ What impact will I have on others when they know that I really listen to them?

➡ What will happen if I don't really listen to people?

➡ How much does it frustrate me when people don't listen to me?

➡ What more can I learn and understand by really listening to people?

These questions might sound a bit contrived and like I am reminding you of the bleeding obvious. Well, sometimes it *is* the bleeding obvious. If we don't remind ourselves of what we already know (i.e., how important it is to really listen to people), then we make it very easy for ourselves to fit the mould and not listen to people. You need to choose to listen and have clear in your mind what it will do for you and those around you, so you make the positive choice in the moment and during your conversations.

So many leaders are going into work telling themselves things like 'I'm really busy' and 'I've got to get X done today' and 'I need to make sure I do Y today'. This stops us from listening, because it fills our mind with busy thoughts, which makes us feel like we haven't got time to listen. Break the mould and tell yourself that you will listen, and why it is so important, and you will create the environment where people want to work.

If you don't understand someone, shut up and listen to them.

2. Talk about LISTENING

This isn't Fight Club; the first rule of LISTENING is to talk about LISTENING! We all know how to do it and we know the value of it, so talk about it with your team. Ask them, 'What do I need to do to show you that I am really listening to you?' And really listen to what they tell you. Then do it!

When you talk about listening and what people expect of you, then you know what you need to do to really listen to them. You don't need to watch TED Talks, do loads of e-learning or go on the latest management development training course to know how to really listen to your team.

Just ask them. When you talk about what it takes for you to really listen to someone, you will learn that they want you to:

➡ Make eye contact

➡ Not be distracted

➡ Not look at your phone or laptop

➡ Talk to them in a quiet space

➡ Summarise and paraphrase what they say

➡ Ask them questions to further explore what they have said

➡ Demonstrate open, positive body language

➡ Show non-verbal cues like nodding and smiling to show that you are listening to them

➡ Empathise with them when they share their personal thoughts and feelings

➡ Not dismiss their ideas or belittle their fears

➡ Not simply turn the topic of conversation round to you

➡ Not rush them – allow for silence when appropriate

➡ Share relevant advice at the right time

➡ Reassure them

➡ Ask how you can help them

➡ Pick up on their non-verbal cues

➡ Give them feedback on how they come across

➡ Follow up on what you talked about

When you talk about listening and then demonstrate the behaviours your team ask of you, you become a much better listener and more motivated to really listen, because you want your team to see you as someone who does what they say they will do. The above isn't an exhaustive list and isn't meant to scare you or phase you; it's a simple list of what people expect from you if you are really LISTENING to them. You have the ability to do all of those things, but you have to choose to do them. Choose the ones from above that you want to work on, and practise them tomorrow. Bring LISTENING into people's awareness in your meetings and one-to-ones. Ask your team to set expectations of each other for how they will listen during your meetings and one-to-ones. This enables you to agree what is expected (e.g., cameras on in video calls, phones and laptops away, don't interrupt each other, make sure everyone gets a chance to talk). When you set those listening expectations, it is much easier to hold each other accountable for really LISTEN-ING and it makes your meetings much more productive, because people listen to each other and leave the conversation with clarity on what happens next.

When people think for themselves, they change their behaviours.

– ADAM KARA

3. Manage the real distractions

To really listen, you need to take care of the real distractions. Yes, put your phone away and yes, close your laptop. More importantly, manage yourself so that you will not be distracted by your thoughts and feelings. It always starts with you.

You can't switch off your heart and mind; even when you are intently listening to someone else, your heart and mind will keep scanning the world and prompting you with thoughts and feelings, alongside all the verbal and non-verbal communication that you are taking in from your conversation partner. That is the distraction you need to manage. The notifications popping up on your phone or another email pinging on your laptop aren't the distraction; the thought that tells you to look at them and the feeling of wanting to know what they say are the distraction. That's what you need to manage.

People who are able to really listen are able to manage their thoughts and feelings and allow them to pass without being taken off course by them. If you set out to really listen to people, why would you let another thought or feeling stop you from achieving it? You can't stop your thoughts and feelings popping up when you're listening – no one on earth can speak as quickly as your brain can process thoughts – but what you can do is choose to allow them to come and go.

When you're listening, see your thoughts and feelings as cars that arrive in front of you and then drive off, clearing the road for you to keep listening. If something really important pops up, make a note of it and come back to it later, at the right time in the conversation. People who interrupt others and jump in to give advice fail to manage the distractions of their thoughts and feelings. They don't love the sound of their own voice, or think they are smarter or more important than you; they just can't manage their own thoughts and feelings.

If you do drift off with your thoughts and feelings and recognise that you have lost your train of listening, then don't give up. Don't tell yourself that you've stopped listening – because people know when you have done that! When you get lost in your thoughts and feelings, you have two choices. The first one is to fess up and tell them that you got distracted and ask them to repeat what they have just said. People value your honesty much more than you trying to pretend you were listening to them, and they will know straight away when you reply with something that has nothing to do with what they just said, or fail to answer the question they asked you. Your second choice is to get back to really listening, and when they stop talking, tell them that you want to summarise what they have just said, to make sure you heard everything correctly. Do just that and give them the chance to correct you, so you can pick up on anything you missed. Everyone you talk to has thoughts and feelings going on when they are listening; you break the mould by choosing to manage those distractions and keep really listening to the person in front of you.

You can practise really listening and managing your distractions. Choose to do it in your conversations tomorrow. Maybe at a meeting when you don't need to actually respond to what someone is saying, spend five minutes just really listening to them – no physical distractions – and practise recognising your thoughts and feelings and allowing them to pass as you keep really listening to the other person. Observe how many thoughts and feelings you experience, and which ones are stronger distractions, and reflect on how you're able to manage those distractions to keep listening. This deliberate practice builds your confidence and ability to really listen when it matters.

All your notifications, emails, thoughts and feelings will still be there when you stop listening to someone. You have to choose to be aware that none of them are more important than what the person in front of you has to say. If you don't choose to really listen, you will never really know what people are thinking.

People don't need a good talking to. They need a good listening to.

– KIRSTY MAC

4. Choose your response

Doing all of the things that people ask you to do while listening will count for nothing if you don't choose to respond in a positive way. Eye contact, non-verbal cues and body language are very important, but what shows the other person that you are really listening to them is how you respond. You don't need to show someone you are listening if your response actually *shows* them that you were listening!

Why the hell were you talking about shorts, Howard?

That was some of the toughest feedback I had to give to a leader I observed having a one-to-one with one of his direct reports. This was part of an Enthuse Your Leadership programme, and one of the key outcomes was for senior leaders to engage in open and engaging one-to-ones with their teams. A key part of this was their ability to really listen. After the development and practice had taken place, I observed the leaders in a real one-to-one that was done remotely. For Howard, a senior operations manager, it was an experience he will probably never forget.

Howard started the one-to-one really well, asking powerful open questions to invite the team member to do the talking, and doing the right things to really listen to them. It was a really engaging conversation; Howard got them talking about one of their ongoing challenges with a customer and exploring their potential solutions. This was where the problem started for Howard. The team member began to talk for a longer period and was visibly really thinking about what they were saying; even on a video call, you could see from their body language and hear from their tone of voice that this was something they found difficult to talk about, and so they naturally took longer to get their words out.

While his team member was challenging themselves and pouring their heart out to a degree, Howard was now choosing to get distracted. He was clearly more interested in what was going on outside his window than he was in what his team member was saying. When his team member finished talking and asked Howard for his views on their ideas, Howard replied very slowly; after a few 'erms' and 'hmms', he responded with, 'So what do you think about all this stuff about shorts?' Then he went on a tirade about how the uniform policy needed changing because he and other managers wanted to wear shorts in the summer months. Not once had his team member mentioned anything about shorts!

The one-to-one quickly descended into a monologue from Howard. His team member shrunk into their chair with a facial expression that told Howard, 'You haven't listened to a word I just said.' Yet Howard was oblivious to that, and wrapped up the conversation with a tick-box exercise of making sure they had talked about everything that was on the form. The team member left the room. It was time for us to go through his feedback.

I first asked Howard how he felt the one-to-one had gone. He told me, in a very non-specific way, that he thought it went OK and that he had definitely listened. I agreed that he had definitely listened during parts of the one-to-one – and then I asked him, 'Why the hell were you talking about shorts, Howard?' Then I gave him feedback based on what I had observed, and had to explain to him how his response about shorts ruined the whole experience for him and his team member. When I asked Howard why he had done that, he said, 'I've heard it all before. I've told him how to sort out that customer, and he keeps coming back with the same thing.' I had made notes of what his team member had said, and when I asked Howard to tell me, he was a million miles from the truth. I took the opportunity to remind him that you never 100% know what someone else is going to say, and the only way to find out is to really listen. When someone is talking to you about something that is important to them, never, ever respond with something that is more important to you!

Howard's example is representative of what is going on in a lot of one-to-ones and shows how easy it is for leaders to get distracted and fall into the trap of thinking that they have to tell people what is on their mind. Choose to listen to what is on your team's minds instead, so they can think for themselves and take responsibility for what happens next. The crazy thing about Howard not choosing to listen in that moment is that he then had to have another conversation about the same issue with the same customer that he was sick of talking about! When you really listen, you give yourself the best chance to resolve issues once and for all.

Most people do not listen with the intent to understand; they listen with the intent to reply.

– STEPHEN COVEY

The ability to really listen comes from practice; the more you practise, the more it becomes part of what you do every day. Use the LISTEN guidance in the *Break the Mould* workbook, which you can find at **www.italwaysstartswithyou.com**, to identify what you need to work on to really listen to your team.

Steve's story:
I have gone back to being me

I want to finish the book by telling you about a leader who inspired me with his determination to change and who encapsulates the purpose of adopting both the Ask, Don't Tell and LISTEN habits. Steve is an executive director of a public sector organisation and broke the mould in a way that others didn't expect; he probably doubted that he could, as well. His story should be the last one you read in this book, because it beautifully captures the importance of breaking the mould. It's a story I love to share with other leaders, and I encourage them to follow Steve's example.

Steve was an exec coaching client of mine who was introduced to me by a sponsor within his people team because they wanted to help him change his behaviour. The picture I was painted when I started working with Steve was that he was entering his last-chance saloon for turning his behaviour around before formal action was taken and a very different outcome pursued. This was backed up when Steve's boss told me, in front of him, that his behaviour had become 'unsavoury and unrecognisable'. The feedback from his team was even more damning and was telling Steve that they weren't going to accept it anymore. Steve sat there listening to this with the air of a naughty schoolboy who knew he was guilty, not at all like the experienced, credible, capable director who led a team of over 50 people that he really was.

At our first meeting, Steve told me that he had been in the business for more than 15 years as a 'man and boy' and was now starting to question his purpose there and wonder what was next for him. Self-doubt had set in, and he was starting to fit the mould that he perceived other directors were fitting into – one of inertia and self-preservation and thinking the world was against them because they were 'the old guard', the senior leaders who were being expected to do the dirty work without any support or recognition. When I asked Steve what he wanted to get from his coaching, he plainly told me with a shrug of the shoulders, 'I don't know. I don't really know why I'm here.'

The fact that Steve went from that to the things he achieved over the 12 months we worked together makes his transformation even more inspirational. As we started to get to know each other better and Steve could see that I wasn't there to (in his words) 'kiss my arse' or 'tell me what to do', he relished the challenges that the coaching presented to him. He set about raising his self-awareness and going back to being who he truly was, reigniting his passion for the work he did. I gave Steve some of the most critical and honest feedback I've ever given to anyone, and he took every bit of it on board and always did something with it. I genuinely sat there thinking 'he's gonna punch me in a minute' after I had shared some observations with him! Thankfully, he never did punch me; instead, he took my feedback away, sought out more feedback from those closest to him, and then at the next session he would absolutely blow me away with what he had done and the impact he was having with his team.

Nobody wants to go to be stuck in a business doing work they hate and don't believe in. Nobody wants to feel that they can't say what they really mean. Yet people choose these things all the time.

– MARK MANSON

To be truly honest, Steve could have approached his coaching with me as a tick-box exercise: showed up, talked the talk, gone away and done some actions, and shown to his boss and the organisation that he was willing to change without really changing anything. Instead, he broke the mould like no one I'd ever seen before and got so far out of his comfort zone, I don't think he'll ever go back in there! What really blew me away with Steve, and what I encourage other leaders to do, was the way he engaged with his team to bring to life what he wanted to achieve, and gave his Ask, Don't Tell and LISTEN habits a life of their own.

Something Steve shared with me during his coaching was that he had lost sight of who he really was. He had been promoted to the director's role to which he had aspired for many years... and suddenly felt lost, unsure of how to behave. He had convinced himself that there was a mould he had to fit into because he was a director, and told himself that he couldn't be his usual jovial, personable self because he now had to be ultra-professional. This had made the fire go out within him and it was taking him away from who he really wanted to be.

The most powerful leadership tool we have is our own example.

– JOHN WOODEN

After Steve had created his Map of the World, I challenged him on how well he knew what his team needed from him and how well he was showing his Map of the World to his direct reports. Steve had three senior managers as his direct reports, two of whom he had long, well-established relationships with and one with whom he had worked for less than 12 months. Steve didn't just ask them what they needed from him; he openly shared with them the coaching he was having, why he was doing it and what he had already learnt about himself. He told them about the mistakes he felt he had made and how committed he was to changing. He shared his Map of the World with them, declaring his intent to go back to his values and be himself. That's breaking the mould right there: an exec leader who tells people who he truly is, openly shares his failings and tells his team what he is doing to fix them.

After Steve shared his own development plan, he then handed each of the three senior managers a handwritten letter in which he shared what he thought he had done well for them and what he would get better at. The letters also contained Steve's praise for the individual managers and told them what they meant to him. He also asked each one of them, 'What do you need from me as your leader to always perform at your best?' The letters triggered transformational conversations with his leadership team, both individually and collectively, that enhanced the trust they had built and enabled them to be open in their feedback to each other.

Each of the managers responded to Steve with their own letter, sharing their personal thoughts and telling him what they needed from him. They also spent time together sharing their Maps of the World and bringing to life what they wanted for themselves and their teams, including realigning their purpose for what they did as a team and the environment they wanted to create.

Be together. Not the same.

Steve did all of that within the first three months of us working together! He was so determined to break the mould, and went from always having his office door closed to working among and with his team. He started to mentor new apprentices in the business and attended community award ceremonies on behalf of his organisation. I remember one session where Steve said to me with beaming pride, 'I have gone back to being me – the Scouse lad from Kirkby.'

Steve achieved his transformation and broke the mould by engaging with the people around him. He stopped hiding away in his office, beating himself up, and got back among them to be his best version of himself. An example that sums this up is that when I first met Steve, we walked together through the office where his team is based. As we walked past the crowded banks of desks, I noticed that Steve stopped chatting to me and kept his head down, not acknowledging anyone around him.

When we returned to his office, I asked him, 'Do you not know anyone out there?'

He replied, 'Yes, of course I do. That's my team'!

I was astonished. 'Why don't you talk to any of them, then?'

That question made Steve think about how he was coming across and triggered change within him. He realised he was creating a perception of himself and telling himself what his team thought of him in a way that wasn't true.

Fast forward six months, and Steve walking through the office was like someone walking through a crowd giving him high fives. He was now introducing me to members of his team and stopping to ask people how they and their families were, putting that famous Scouse sense of humour to good use by taking the mickey out of the women on his team for having their rollers in at work! He now never shut his office door unless it was for a private meeting, and hanging from said door was a wheel of fortune that Steve had created. On it were prizes such as a lottery ticket, a day off and even a free week's stay at Steve's holiday villa in Spain! Steve had set this up himself and, every month, the team chose a colleague to spin the wheel and win one of the prizes.

Steve achieved so much of his positive change by spending his time with people, asking them powerful open questions and really listening to them. He went back to showing people the decent human being that he is. As a result, everything changed for the better for Steve, his team and the business.

People will forgive lots for people who bring them joy.

– JIMMY MURPHY

Let's give Steve himself the final word for how to break the mould.

I approached my coaching journey with Tim with mixed emotions. I knew I had to do something to shake me out of the leadership lethargy I had allowed myself to fall into, but what could I learn from this guy? He didn't know me, and he didn't know anything about the challenges I faced.

Over the months I worked with Tim, our sessions didn't feel like something I had been told to do but something I looked forward to doing. It became like meeting your mate for a weekly drink in the local pub. The type of friend, though, that shines a light on your bullshit and makes you think about how you could become your best version of yourself. I've always striven to be better today than I was yesterday, and I'd lost that drive a little prior to working with Tim. He helped me rediscover my passion for my work, my people, and rediscover my purpose. Thanks, Tim— keep cutting through the bullshit and helping people find themselves and what inspires them.

You don't need a manager's toolkit or a supermodel to help you to be a better leader; just be more like Steve and break the mould in your own authentic way.

I'm gonna keep our eyes on
Looking for the good times
Trying to stay high on (high on)
Looking for the glad times
Gonna get my head up
Looking for the good times
Biding my time
Waiting for the glad times.

– PAUL WELLER

How does LISTENING help you break the mould?

➡ It empowers you to choose to LISTEN.

➡ You find out what's really going on for people.

➡ You get to understand and learn from other people to inform how you positively respond to them.

➡ People are surrounded by people who don't listen to them. When you really listen to them it shows them that you are a leader who can be trusted and someone they want to work for.

CHAPTER 12

WHAT ARE YOU GOING TO DO ABOUT IT?

That is the most important question to consider as a result of reading this book. Don't let it become something else that you've done and don't do anything with! Leaders who are happy to fit the mould are the ones who learn something about themselves but deny themselves the chance to do something with it. If you've enjoyed this book, before you put it down, identify the key steps you are going to take to break the mould.

Let's remind you of the key learnings of this book:

➡ What people really want from you is your true, authentic self.

➡ You are not your job; you are you.

➡ Your power comes from being your best version of you.

➡ Leadership is not about a style, model or theory; it's about you.

➡ You have to sort your own shit out first before you can help others.

➡ No decent human being was ever made from corporate bullshit.

➡ There are lots of dickheads out there – you need to choose not to be one of them.

➡ Your Map of the World is the key to authentic leadership.

➡ You have to get to know and master your self-talk.

➡ Don't moan about it – get on with it.

➡ Keep the nobheads in their own circle.

➡ Ask, Don't Tell.

➡ LISTENING is not a skill; it is a choice.

➡ It always starts with you.

So what are you going to do about it? The best thing might be to tell other people about it and give this book to someone else who needs to break the mould. Or is it about changing your beliefs about leadership, dropping the styles and supermodels and replacing them with your true, authentic self? It could be that my story resonated with you the most and you need to find what you're supposed to be doing and ignite your passion for leadership. Maybe it will be all about living up to what you stand for or mastering your self-talk. Perhaps you can't wait to talk to your team about your No-Moan Zone or create your Circle of Nobheads. Or are you excited to practise asking open questions and being able to really listen to people and see what positive difference that makes for you? Whatever has resonated with you from reading this book, make sure that you do something with it – because the most basic, simplest way to break the mould is to do something with what you learn.

Three final questions to consider:

➡ What is the first thing you are going to do to break the mould?

➡ What will you be doing in six months to break the mould?

➡ How will you make sure that you never fit the moulds others set for you?

There are some more questions in the *Break the Mould* workbook that will help you to do something with this book. So, if you have come this far without downloading it, don't go any further without it; head to **www.italwaysstartswithyou.com** and grab your copy before it's too late.

Let's stay together – connect and subscribe

Don't let the book be the only thing we do together. I am a real person, not some ghost writer or a publisher's pseudonym! If you like the stories and ideas I have shared, then there are plenty more where they came from. I had to choose which ones to share here with you, because my publisher will only let me put so many words in one book! There is so much more that I do with coaching clients and leadership teams. You ain't seen anything until you have seen me deliver an inspirational talk – your conference or event will never be the same again once it's been Enthused. Remember that I have to keep the book relatively general and at a higher level. When we work together– especially one-to-one or with you and your team– we can do so much more, either with a deep dive into your true, authentic self and the leader you want to be or by creating bespoke tailored solutions for you and your team.

Connect with me and get in touch via LinkedIn (**https://www.linkedin.com/in/timrobertsenthuse/**) to show me how you are breaking the mould. Sign up to my LinkedIn

Break the Mould newsletter and join my LinkedIn Live sessions. I'd love to see your pictures with the book and hear how it is making a difference to you and helping you to be your true, authentic self. Tag me and **#italwaysstartswithyou** in your pictures of you and your team working together to create your Map of the World, No-Moan Zone and Circle of Nobheads.

Subscribe at **www.enthusecoaching.com**, where you will join other fans of Enthuse who get more ideas for how to break the mould via monthly videos, blogs and real-life stories. I also share free downloads for more practical ideas on how to be the leader you want to be. My online events are where you can be yourself in a safe space and meet others who refuse to be what others tell them to be. Subscribers also get exclusive pre-sale access to my online tours.

Scan the QR code below to head to my website where you can subscribe:

How to work with me

One-to-one coaching

The most powerful way to break the mould. We work together to give you the space to get clarity on your true, authentic self. As your Enthuse Coach, I will create the environment for you to raise your self-awareness and make positive choices. I have created 6- and 12-month coaching programmes for you to choose from, or you can have me on a retainer for your VIP bespoke coaching needs (or, as one client put it, 'I just need to lock you in a cupboard, Tim, that I can open every day when I need you'!) and we meet as and when you need me for as long as you need me. I'll challenge you to think differently and to come up with your own powerful solutions. I'll support you all the way and give you the feedback that you need to hear so you can be your best version of you.

Tim is by far (in my opinion) the greatest coach there is! It's actually quite hard to put into words how much Tim's coaching has helped me, but I will try... He has not only helped me to shut down my BS Factory (aka imposter syndrome), lack of confidence, shying away from being brave, but he has also helped me to find out what my true passions in life are. With that, we've been able to work through a number of sce-

narios that ensure I am constantly working towards my goals of being the best version of me, and I know what will make me happy. If you want a coach who is knowledgeable, inspiring, honest, has a great taste in music, and is energetic, empathetic and (a bit) funny— then Tim is the coach for you!

– AMY MILNER, HEAD OF TALENT

Enthuse Your Leadership

I work with organisations and leadership teams to get their leaders enthused. This is leadership development that takes a coaching approach to break the mould. My Enthuse learning experiences are anything but boring, and if you think it's death by PowerPoint, then you have my permission to kill me on the spot. It includes a six-month development programme that takes leadership teams through a combination of interactive learning experiences, one-to-one coaching and verbatim feedback— or we can build your programme together to suit your unique needs.

If you want more of a short, sharp impact, then my Enthuse Your Leadership events can be done over one or two days. These are a mix of group coaching and inspirational talks and can be run for up to 50 leaders at a time to bring people together and leave a lasting impact on them. I also offer Enthuse learning experiences that cover a variety of topics, so you can develop yourself and your leaders in specific areas of leadership. These are available in bite-sized, half-day or one-day sessions.

All leadership development experiences are best in person, where we can see the whites of each other's eyes and get some real energy going. But I am also a dab hand at talking to a laptop and can support you virtually if that's your thing, or because it's the best way to reach a global audience, as some of my clients ask me to do for them.

Just being around Tim is intuitive, insightful and always inspiring! We worked with Tim to bring emotional intelligence and positive mindset into our conversations across multiple levels of our company. Tim shared his expertise within this area by a series of events and workshops. We began with the senior leadership team, followed this with an all-company event and then worked with our managers to embed an approach where we facilitate a positive mindset in others from within our culture. As standalone sessions they were really great. As a series Tim was able to share so much more with us, really taking the time to understand our organisation and support what makes us who we are. I would highly recommend working with Tim; he is a real expert in his field.

— LYDIA KENNEDY, HEAD OF PEOPLE

Enthuse Inspirational Talks

Get me to speak at your conference or event. My no-bullshit approach to speaking is guaranteed to light up a room and get people talking. I am no stranger to big audiences and make an impact with humour, straight talking and practical ideas to get you inspired. Book me as your keynote speaker for an experience that people will never forget. I have three good-to-go talks that I can do for you tomorrow, or I can write a bespoke talk that works best for your audience and the purpose of your event. I also work as an MC at large conferences and events and can promise you that I will make your event even better than it has been with my engaging hosting and speaker introductions that ignite the room.

Unique, courageous and highly emotionally intelligent, Tim is one of the finest examples of inspirational speakers I have had the privilege of working with.

Blending humility with his energetic high-drive style and seeking to leave every coachee, team or audience filled with passion and compelled to act, he can engage you on a personal and professional level instantly. Whatever the challenge your organisation faces, let Tim be a part of the solution.

– JULIA DARVILL, MANAGING DIRECTOR

Enthuse Online Tours

The best thing to come out of Covid-induced lockdowns! In 2020 I created my Enthuse Tours, which provide a safe and creative online space for you to be yourself. My tours are group coaching programmes, and they include free events and paid-for tickets that give you a coaching programme for 6–12 months where you can work with your peers. Let's be honest – not everyone can afford one-to-one coaching, and not everyone works somewhere that invests in them. My online tours offer development opportunities like no other, and all at an affordable ticket price. Not only do they offer you access to exclusive content and coaching, but I also play some quality tunes and give you the chance to build your network.

Full of great music, great laughs but most importantly great content, Tim is an incredibly engaging speaker, a no-nonsense approach with a huge slice of emo-

tional intelligence that is a breath of fresh air. The Enthuse Tour is a welcome break from the day-to-day to really reflect and engage. Tim truly cares for his audience and creating change in how we tackle real business or personal challenges through coaching and authenticity. Sign up, be present, be you.

— FAY DIXON, LEARNING AND DEVELOPMENT PARTNER

Head to **www.enthusecoaching.com** now to download my Enthuse setlists and find out which Enthuse solution will help you best to break the mould.

Keep smiling. Keep being you.

That's all I ever meant
That's the message that I sent
I can't give everything
I can't give everything away.

— DAVID BOWIE

MY TOP 10 BOOKS TO HELP YOU TO BREAK THE MOULD

Seven Habits of Highly Effective People by Stephen Covey

Man's Search for Meaning by Victor Frankl

Fierce Conversations by Susan Scott

Emotional Intelligence by Daniel Goleman

How to Win Friends and Influence People by Dale Carnegie

Absolute Beginners by Colin MacInnes

Life Will See You Now by Gavin Oattes

The Life-Changing Magic of Not Giving a Fuck by Sarah McKnight

The Tattooist of Auschwitz by Heather Morris

Tuesdays with Morrie by Mitch Albom

MY TOP 10 RECORDS TO HELP YOU TO BREAK THE MOULD

Hunky Dory by David Bowie

Exile on Main Street by The Rolling Stones

What's Going On by Marvin Gaye

True Meanings by Paul Weller

All Mod Cons by The Jam

Love and Hate by Michael Kiwanuka

Definitely Maybe by Oasis

Let It Be by The Beatles

The Universal Want by Doves

Back to Black by Amy Winehouse

Listen to my Break The Mould Spotify playlist here:

ACKNOWLEDGEMENTS

I have to start by showing my gratitude to my family – Mum, Dad & 'our kid' Claire. Thank you for your love and for giving me an understanding of the world. And for showing me that having manners, always having a laugh, and treating your friends right are more important than anything else in this world.

Unsurprisingly I next have to go for the musicians who have inspired me and kept me going through the good times and bad times. Many of them are referenced in the book and extra special mentions have to go to Paul Weller and David Bowie, without whom my mental health struggles would have been much, much worse. And to Oasis, who kicked it all off for me in the 90s (I still want to be Liam Gallagher!).

To all the authors who have inspired me – thank you. Thank you for giving a shit about other people and getting off your arse and giving your books to the world. I love reading, it's one of life's gifts. Anyone can sit and stare at a television or laptop screen. People who read choose to want to know more about the world, to be curious and to learn more about themselves. Whatever you think of self-help or personal development or leadership books (who cares what we call them?!), they are there for you to explore and to make you think differently. I've read hundreds of them already and every new one gives me something else to inspire me. There is always a different way to think about things and you always have the power to choose your attitudes and behaviours and books are the key to doing just that.

I can't write my first book without mentioning Stephen Covey, Daniel Goleman, Viktor Frankl, Heather Morris, Sarah Knight, Brene Brown, Mitch Albom, Gavin Oattes, Dale Carnegie, Seth Godin, Michael Bungay Stanier and Daniel Kahneman. And many, many more! Thank you.

Before I acknowledge all the people, who have inspired me, I want to say a thank you to all the dickheads out there. Without you this book would never have been written. You motivate me to be better every day; to never adopt a negative mindset and to not behave in a way that just isn't me. And most importantly to never, ever be a dickhead! Without your narcissism, your discrimination, your ignorance, your patronising, your lies, your lack of humility and self-awareness and your general dickheadedness, I would never have had to look for another way to lead and to explore what it really means to be my true, authentic self. So, thank you to the dickheads for making a life a misery during the times we spent together and for making sure that I will always have a job to do helping people to not be like you!

To the people who have inspired me and helped me to write this book, I can't thank you enough. For whatever reason you have chosen to give me your time, to listen to me, to share your wisdom with me, to challenge me and to just be there for me, I am eternally grateful. Writing a book is the one lifetime ambition I have always had, and you have helped me to achieve that. Working with people like you has made me realise that you can't actually do anything alone. Yes, it always starts with you, and you have to make connections with others and build relationships with the people who make you better (no nobheads allowed remember!). So in the most boring bullet point kind of way possible, I want to say particular thanks to: -

➡ **Leila Green.** You have to be first on the list Leila. This book literally wouldn't exist without you. How I deserved you as my writing coach is beyond me. You pulled me back from the brink and motivated me on countless occasions. You listened to my waffle and always made me believe that I could do it even when what I had written was shit! You called out the bullshit and made sure that I wrote it as me and refused to accept anything else which is the biggest compliment anyone can receive. Thank you Leila – are you ready for volume two?!

➡ **Martin Hesketh** for believing in me and giving me my first leadership position. Your years of mentorship have meant so much to me and I still ask myself *'what would MJH tell me to do?'*!

➡ **Rob Johnson and Karene Lamond** for being my mentors and making me believe that I could be a coach and inspirational speaker. You have shared so much with me and challenged me which has made me think that all this is possible. I will never forget the laughs we've had and your encouragement to do this job that we love as nothing else but our true, authentic selves.

➡ **Danny Seals.** It feels like a Tinder kind of relationship seeing as we met online and have been hitting it off ever since! You are a legend, my friend, and the way you bring people together shows the world that hope is never lost.

➡ **Aimee Bateman.** Where would I be without you kicking my arse when I need it Aimee? Always there to support me, always there to make me laugh and always there to help me see things differently. And your immortal line that made me realise that I can just be me... *"you are not everyone's cup of tea Tim. Embrace that and use it to be even better than you already are."*

→ **Zoe Jones** (the leader formally known as Zoe Sinclair!). Always honest (remember when you called me boring?!), always personable, always inspirational, always challenging me, always Zoe. Imagine if I'd never got to work with you?! God, my career would be boring. Thank you for showing me that there is another way and that I don't have to follow the dickheads.

→ **Jo Wright.** One day we'll have a podcast series that is just me and you putting the world to rights... And it will be an international best seller! Thanks for trusting me to lead with Coaching Culture, thanks for believing in me, thanks for being as passionate about coaching as I am. Thanks for being you.

→ **(my mate) Jules Darvill.** The one and only Jules who is the most authentic senior leader there is. Thanks for making me laugh from the minute we met, thanks for sending me the tunes every week, thanks for reminding me to always make time for me. Thanks for not giving a fuck about the things that don't matter and standing on stage captivating hundreds of people with your honesty.

→ **Nova Ferguson.** First of all, thank you for somehow putting up with me being the only one on my Coaching Qualification all those years ago!! Thanks for asking me coaching questions that have included Fred Perry, Paul Weller and Keith Richards! You are the best coach on earth, and I feel immensely lucky to have you as my coach and a friend.

So many other people and not enough pages left! Honourable mentions go to Martin McGhee, Bethany Lang, Gee Atkinson, Lauren Hamilton, Shaun Lanceley, Lisa Gritton, Mark Leach, Jo Byrne and Loiza Tallon who either gave up their time for free to help me with Enthuse or who put their trust in me when Enthuse first launched. To everyone who contributed to the testimonials at the start of the book, thank you for taking your time to help me and give it a great first impression!

To all of my coaching clients, the leaders I have worked with, the audience members at my talks and those of you who have joined my tours. Thanks for being there and thank you for giving me the chance to do the job that I love. This book is an ode to you for inspiring me and giving me the stories to tell. And for those of you who will be my clients in the future – I'm ready when you are for you to be *your* best version of you.

You're the best thing...

The book started with you, and it ends with you – Joyno, Phoebe, Lucie and Dusty, you are the best thing that ever happened to me. Thank you for putting up with me. Thank you for letting me take over our house with my vinyl records and books. Thank you for never doubting me. Thank you for never making me fit a mould or give up on my dreams. Thank you for not repeating my swearing. Thank you for making me laugh (especially at myself). Thank you for making sure that I never believe my own hype and that I never turn into something that I am not. If you like this book and it makes you proud of me then it has all been worth it.

Keep smiling. Keep being you.

#ITALWAYSSTARTSWITHYOU

Lightning Source UK Ltd.
Milton Keynes UK
UKHW011011230622
404853UK00002B/83